The Old Testament Basis of Christian Apologetics

The Old Testament Basis of Christian Apologetics

A Biblical-Theological Survey

SIEGBERT RIECKER

WIPF & STOCK · Eugene, Oregon

THE OLD TESTAMENT BASIS OF CHRISTIAN APOLOGETICS
A Biblical-Theological Survey

Copyright © 2018 Siegbert Riecker. All rights reserved. Except for brief quotations in critical publications or reviews, no part of this book may be reproduced in any manner without prior written permission from the publisher. Write: Permissions, Wipf and Stock Publishers, 199 W. 8th Ave., Suite 3, Eugene, OR 97401.

Wipf & Stock
An Imprint of Wipf and Stock Publishers
199 W. 8th Ave., Suite 3
Eugene, OR 97401

www.wipfandstock.com

PAPERBACK ISBN: 978-1-5326-7262-0
HARDCOVER ISBN: 978-1-5326-7263-7
EBOOK ISBN: 978-1-5326-7264-4

Manufactured in the U.S.A.   NOVEMBER 28, 2018

Scripture quotations are from New Revised Standard Version Bible, copyright © 1989 National Council of the Churches of Christ in the United States of America. Used by permission. All rights reserved worldwide. http://nrsvbibles.org

Scripture references according to the Hebrew Bible. In square brackets deviating verse numbering in the New Revised Standard Version.

Contents

Preface | vii

Abbreviations | ix

Introduction: A Missing Foundation | xii

    1. What Do We Understand by Apologetics? | 1

    2. Apologetics and Biblical Theology | 19

    3. Genesis 1:1–2:3 Between Polemics and Apologetics | 30

    4. Narrative Apologetics | 36

    5. Prophetic Apologetics | 47

    6. Wisdom Apologetics | 60

    7. Citatory Apologetics as Antithetic Proclamation | 70

    8. Exemplary Apologetics | 86

    9. Apologetics as Challenge and Mandate | 88

Bibliography | 93

Preface

IN THE YEAR 2013, I started writing a short introductory chapter to a textbook on apologetics, dealing with the biblical-theological foundations of the discipline.[1] What stunned me back then was the fact that there was virtually no reference to the Old Testament in the published literature dealing with that theme so far. It surprised me even more because in one of the introductory chapters[2] to my dissertation, presented in 2006,[3] I was able to draw on an abundance of articles and even books dealing with the Old Testament basis of missions. Every proper biblical-theological foundation in the discipline of missiology has to deal with the Old Testament or at least justify the abstinence from doing so.[4] Why was the Old Testament so important for missions and yet so seemingly insignificant as a basis for apologetics? Was there a categorical difference between the discipline of apologetics and the discipline of missiology that I had missed?

When we look in the New Testament, we observe that Paul usually does not need the gospels to defend the gospel. Only very rarely does he even need to refer to an actual word spoken by his

---

1. Riecker, "Exegetische Begründung," 23–37.

2. This chapter was eventually published in 2008 in a more elaborate form as *Mission im Alten Testament? Ein Forschungsüberblick mit Auswertung*.

3. Published in 2007 as *Ein Priestervolk für alle Völker: Der Segensauftrag Israels für alle Nationen in der Tora und den Vorderen Propheten*. Some of its results are represented in my English article "Missions in Hebrew Bible," 324–39.

4. Amongst others, the chapter by Michael A. Grisanti with the ominous title: "The Missing Mandate: Missions in the Old Testament," 43–68.

savior Jesus. For sure, one reason for this phenomenon is that he finds enough solid ground in the Old Testament to substantiate his message. This strengthens his case especially in confrontation with his Jewish opponents. What he defends is not just a possible fabrication of his controversial messiah, but the sacred tradition of the chosen people of Israel. In the Old Testament, Paul not only finds reason for the message, but also a cause for his mission. Could he not also find a cause there for the task of apologetics?

Whereas it seems quite unlikely that the Old Testament has so little to say about a topic of such clear importance, it becomes even more unlikely if we take into consideration the fact that apologetics is not only one individual theme but a broader field including further aspects of faith. When I could not get this question out of my mind, I started an investigation the results of which were sketched in a concise article published in 2016.[5]

This book presents the results of this investigation on a broader basis. On the one hand it is intended to fill a gap, on the other hand to initiate a discussion about the significance of a biblical-theological investigation of the Old Testament for the establishment of Christian apologetics.

I would like to give special thanks to Wendy Schulte and her husband Steffen from Wölmersen, as well as Billy and Jennie Dale from Eastbourne, East Sussex, for their continuous support and patience throughout the editing and writing process of this manuscript.

---

5. Riecker, "Alttestamentliche Grundlagen," 1–27.

Abbreviations

AB	The Anchor Bible
ABD	*The Anchor Bible Dictionary*, edited by David Noel Freedman (New York, NY: Doubleday, 1992)
AnBib	Analecta biblica
ATANT	Abhandlungen zur Theologie des Alten und Neuen Testaments
ATD	Das Alte Testament Deutsch
ATM	Altes Testament und Moderne
AUSS	*Andrews University Seminary Studies*
AYBRL	Anchor Yale Bible Reference Library
BAFCS	The Book of Acts in Its First Century Setting
BBB	Bonner Biblische Beiträge
BEATAJ	Beiträge zur Erforschung des Alten Testaments und des Antiken Judentums
BET	Beiträge zur biblischen Exegese und Theologie
BETL	Bibliotheca Ephemeridum theologicarum Lovaniensium
BETS	Bulletin of the Evangelical Theological Society
BhEvTh	Beihefte zur evangelischen Theologie
BIS	Biblical Interpretation Series
BKAT	Biblischer Kommentar. Altes Testament
BN	*Biblische Notizen*
BS	*Bibliotheca Sacra*
BSt	Biblische Studien

BWANT	Beiträge zur Wissenschaft vom Alten und Neuen Testament
BZAW	Beihefte zur Zeitschrift für die alttestamentliche Wissenschaft
BZNW	Beihefte zur Zeitschrift für die neutestamentliche Wissenschaft
BZ, NF	*Biblische Zeitschrift, Neue Folge*
CBQ	*Catholic Biblical Quarterly*
CThM	Calwer theologische Monographien
DOTW	*Dictionary of the Old Testament: Wisdom, Poetry & Writings*, edited by Tremper Longman III, and Peter Enns (Leicester: InterVarsity, 2008)
EBR	*Encyclopedia of the Bible and its Reception*, edited by Hans-Joseph Klauck und Dale C. Allison (Berlin: De Gruyter, 2009ff)
EnAC	Entreties sur l'Antiquité classique de la Fondation Hardt
EWNT	*Exegetisches Wörterbuch zum Neuen Testament*, edited by Horst Balz and Gerhard Schneider (Stuttgart: Kohlhammer, 1980–1983, ²1992, ³2011)
EQ	*Evangelical Quarterly*
FAT	Forschungen zum Alten Testament
FOTL	The Forms of the Old Testament Literature
FRLANT	Forschungen zur Religion und Literatur des Alten und Neuen Testaments
FzB	Forschungen zur Bibel
HCOT	Historical Commentary on the Old Testament
HST	Handbuch Systematische Theologie
HThR	*Harvard Theological Review*
JBTh	Jahrbuch für biblische Theologie
JETh	*Jahrbuch für Evangelikale Theologie*
JETS	*Journal of the Evangelical Theological Society*
JSOT	*Journal for the Study of the Old Testament*
JSOT.S	Journal for the Study of the Old Testament Supplement Series

KAT	Kommentar zum Alten Testament
KeH	Kurzgefasstes exegetisches Handbuch
KuD	*Kerygma und Dogma*
Lang. Soc.	*Language in Society*
LThK³	*Lexikon für Theologie und Kirche*, edited by Walter Kasper et al., 3rd edition (Freiburg: Herder, 1993-2001)
MThZ	*Münchener Theologische Zeitschrift*
NCB	The New Century Bible Commentary
NKZ	*Neue kirchliche Zeitschrift*
NTS	*New Testament Studies*
RE³	*Realencyklopädie für protestantische Theologie und Kirche*, edited by Albert Hauck, 3rd edition (Leipzig: J.C. Hinrich'sche Buchhandlung, 1896-1913)
RestQ	*Restoration Quarterly*
RGG³	*Die Religion in Geschichte und Gegenwart. Handwörterbuch für Theologie und Religionswissenschaft*, edited by Kurt Galling, 3rd edition (Tübingen: J.C.B. Mohr, 1957-1965)
RGG⁴	*Religion in Geschichte und Gegenwart. Handwörterbuch für Theologie und Religionswissenschaft*, edited by Hans Dieter Betz, 4th edition (Tübingen: Mohr Siebeck, 1998-2007)
SBB	Stuttgarter Biblische Beiträge
SIHC	Studies in the Intercultural History of Christianity
SNTS.MS	Society for New Testament Studies Monograph Series
StANT	Studien zum Alten und Neuen Testament
STAR	Studies in Theology and Religion
THAT	*Theologisches Handwörterbuch zum Alten Testament*, edited by Ernst Jenni und Claus Westermann (Gütersloh: Kaiser, 1971/1975, ⁵1994/⁴1993)
ThR	*Theologische Rundschau*

TRE	*Theologische Realenzyklopädie*, edited by Gerhard Krause (until vol. 12) and Gerhard Müller (Berlin: De Gruyter, 1977–2004)
OBO	Orbis Biblicus et Orientalis
OTL	The Old Testament Library
Sem.	*Semitica*
USQR	*Union Seminary Quarterly Review*
VT	*Vetus Testamentum*
VT.S	Supplements to Vetus Testamentum
WBC	Word Biblical Commentary
WMANT	Wissenschaftliche Monographien zum Alten und Neuen Testament
WUNT	Wissenschaftliche Untersuchungen zum Neuen Testament
ZBK	Zürcher Bibelkommentare
ZKTh	*Zeitschrift für katholische Theologie*
ZThK	*Zeitschrift für Theologie und Kirche*
ZAW	*Zeitschrift für die Alttestamentliche Wissenschaft*
ZNW	*Zeitschrift für die Neutestamentliche Wissenschaft und die Kunde der älteren Kirche*
ZRG	*Zeitschrift für Religions- und Geistesgeschichte*

Introduction
A Missing Foundation

THE DISCIPLINE OF CHRISTIAN apologetics is traditionally based on a biblical-theological investigation. The same is true for the discipline of Christian missiology. A textbook on mission sciences is usually expected to include a survey of "sending" passages in the Old Testament at the outset, and discuss the question of how far a concept of missions can be found in the Hebrew Scriptures.[1] However, in the realm of Christian apologetics, the Old Testament is only rarely considered when apologists look for a biblical vindication of their task. Certainly, the Old Testament has a most prominent and honorable place as an *object* of modern Christian apologetics—if we only consider the innumerable studies on the credibility and historical reliability of the creation account, miracles, and the ancient biblical reports. However, little is expected of the Old Testament as *rationale* of the discipline.

A New Testament theology of apologetics is well developed and made accessible through many articles and reference works.[2]

---

1. Regarding the current state of research, see Jongeneel, *Philosophy*, 107–16; Scheurer, *Altes Testament und Mission*; Okoye, *Israel and Nations*, 5–9; Riecker, *Mission*.

2. See Wernle, "Altchristliche Apologetik," 42–65; Scott, *Apologetic of New Testament*; Heffern, *Apology and Polemic*; Nestle, "Zur altchristlichen Apologetik," 115–23; Kamlah, "Apologetik I," 477–80; Bruce, *Apostolic Defence*; Reid, "Apologetic Elements," 15–35; Dulles, "Apologetics," 1–21; Stanton, "Aspects," 377–92; Droge, "Apologetics," 302–7; Lüdemann, "Apologetik III," 614–6; Vos, *Kunst der Argumentation*; Omerzu, "Apologetics III," 426–31. Lampe and

INTRODUCTION

The area of New Testament apologetics is typically broken down into four reconstructed frontlines:

- Defense against Judaism
- Defense against paganism
  (Greek-Roman religion and philosophy)
- Defense against the Roman empire (secular authorities)
- Defense against intrusion of foreign teaching
  (inner-church polemics)

Textbooks on Christian apologetics as well as theological dictionaries[3] usually start with the New Testament. An Old Testament theology of apologetics however has only rarely been developed. In his recent survey, *Mapping Apologetics,* Brian Morley dedicates two and a half pages to "identify some general themes" in the Old Testament, but is not able to utilize any existing resources. He introduces this short passage with the telling words: "Much more work needs to be done on the subject of apologetics in the Bible, especially in the Old Testament." [4]

At first glance, this observed deficit might be based on the fact that an Old Testament equivalent to the *locus classicus* of Apologetics is not easily detected:

> Always be ready to make your defense to anyone who demands from you an accounting for the hope that is in you (1 Pet 3:15).

Samley, *Paul and Rhetoric*; Stenschke, "Apologetik, Polemik und Mission," 244–53.

3. Rare exceptions are Seckler, "Apologetik I," 834–36; Seckler, "Apologetik II," 836 with seven lines of text referring to the Old Testament; Levinson, "Apologetik 1," 47, with two paragraphs referring to the Old Testament; Hinson, "Apologetics, Biblical," 29–30, with one and a half column; and Chazan, "Apologetics II," 416, with three paragraphs referring to the Old Testament.

4. Morley, *Mapping Apologetics,* 29. On pp. 29–31 he refers to Deut 18:21–22, 28:1–14; Josh 2:9–11; 1 Sam 2:30; 1 Kgs 17:24, 18:39, 20:23, 28; 2 Kgs 2:13; Isa 37, 40:18–20, 41:6–7, 11–12, 17–21, 23, 29, 43:26, 44:9–20, 45:20–21, 46:2, 7, 10, 49:23; Jer 14:22; Hab 2:18; Ps 18:26, 115:4–8, 135,15–18, and Job. However, there are no annotations with references to any further literature.

INTRODUCTION

Where in the Old Testament can we find such a clear reference to apologetics?

Methodologically, but also from a historical perspective, this shortcoming can hardly be justified. The pre-Constantinian anonymous *Epistle to Diognetus*—dated by many in the second or third century CE by others even earlier—exemplifies the great value of the Old Testament for Christian apologetics from the outset. The first three of the original ten chapters of this apologetic letter are heavily dependent on idol polemic passages in the Old Testament prophets and beyond.[5]

Looking further back to the time of Jesus and the apostles, Barnabas Lindars and others have convincingly pointed out the vital role of the Old Testament in New Testament apologetics itself.[6]

---

5. Especially Diog 2,1–10; 3,3–5. See Jefford, *Epistle to Diognetus*.

6. See particularly Lindars, *New Testament Apologetic*; Ferguson, "Apologetics," 189–96, as well as most of the above-mentioned books and papers on New Testament apologetics referring to the apologetic use of the Old Testament within the New Testament.

1

What Do We Understand by Apologetics?

ETYMOLOGICAL CONSIDERATIONS

IN ORDER TO INVESTIGATE an Old Testament mandate or rationale of apologetics, it is important to be aware of the exact concept one is looking for. Etymologically the word 'apologetics' derives from the Greek noun *apología* (verb *apologéomai*). Initially these expressions are used in ancient rhetoric to denote a speech for the defense on trial. The apology is the counterpart to the prosecution speech, the *katēgoría* "accusation" (noun), or *katēgoréō* "to accuse" (verb). In this regard these terms also occur in the *Apology of Socrates* by Plato which could have had a role-modeling influence on early Christian defense literature: "It is right for me, gentlemen, to defend myself *[apologēsasthai]* first against the first lying accusations *[katēgoreména]* made against me and my first accusers *[katēgórous]*, and then against the later . . ."[1]

---

1. Plato (ca. 427–347 BCE), *Apology* 18a. Grube, "Apology," 19. First records of the terms already with the teacher of rhetoric Antiphon of Rhamnus (ca. 480–411 BCE), *Orationes* 5,8 and 6,7, later amongst others with the historian Thucydides (ca. 460–395 BCE), Aristotle (384–322 BCE), *Rhetoric* 1,3, see Barnard, "Apologetik I," 373, and further records with Fiedrowicz, *Apologie*, 18. Liddell et al., *A Greek-English Lexicon*, 207.

The equivalent pair of opposites occurs four times in the New Testament referring to lawsuits of Jews against Paul.[2] Furthermore, Paul thinks in *katēgoroúnton* and *apologouménōn* categories when he reflects on the heart and conscience of the non-Jewish unbeliever:

> [The gentiles] show that what the law requires is written on their hearts, to which their own conscience also bears witness; and their conflicting thoughts will accuse or perhaps excuse them (Rom 2:15).

The only synoptic gospel to use the verb *apologéomai* is the Gospel of Luke. If Christians are taken to court, they are assured of God's spiritual support:

> When they bring you before the synagogues, the rulers, and the authorities, do not worry about how you are to defend yourselves *[apologḗsesthe]* or what you are to say; for the Holy Spirit will teach you at that very hour what you ought to say (Luke 12:11, 21:14).

Nevertheless, they have to be willing outside of court to make their *apología* "defense" to anyone who demands it from them (1 Pet 3:15).

A closer look at the use of *katēgoréō* within the gospels[3] reveals that only a fraction of thematically associated texts can be identified by limiting the search to the root *apologéomai*. The related opposing pair *katēgoréō* and *apokrínomai* also occurs frequently within the gospels.[4]

---

2. Acts 22:1, v. 30; 24:10, v. 2; 8; 13; 19; 25:8, v. 11; 25:16, v. 16; and 18–19. Further occurrences of the root *apolog*—in connection with the trials of Paul: Acts 19:33, 26:1, 2, 24; Phil 1:7, 16; and 2 Tim 4:16. In connection with his dispute with the Corinthians: 1 Cor 9:3; and 2 Cor 7:11, 12:19. In total *apología* appears in the New Testament eight times, and *apologéomai* ten times. See Kellermann, "*apologeomai*," 329–30, Aland, *Apologie*, 22–24.

3. Matt 12:10, 27:12; Mark 3:2, 15:3, 4; Luke 6:7, 23:2, 10, 14; and John 5:45, 8:6; *katēgoría*: 18:29.

4. Matt 27:12; Mark 15:4, see 11:29, 14:60–61, 15:2; Luke 17:20, 23:3, 9; and John 1:21.

What Do We Understand by Apologetics?

Furthermore, it does not seem reasonable to narrow down the concept of "apologetics" to the meaning of "defense" by means of an etymological derivation, even if one takes into account other synonymous terms and related Bible passages.[5] From a semantic perspective, the concept of "defense" can be subsumed under the category of communication, where a number of other apologetically relevant concepts can be detected, such as explaining, discussing, testifying, criticizing, debating, arguing, or objecting.[6]

The designation "apologists" was introduced by patristic scholars Fédéric Morel (1552–1630) and Prudent Maran (1683–1762) to refer to a group of Christian Greek authors in the second century CE. "Classic" early Christian apologists include Aristides of Athens, Justin Martyr, Athenagoras of Athens, Apollinaris Claudius, Melito of Sardes, and Tertullian, as well as others. Their work can be understood as a substitute for the often refused defense of their accused Christian brothers and sisters. The early Christian apologists did not only vindicate their faith against accusations (defensive) but also pointed out mistakes and weaknesses of their opponents (offensive) and presented the Christian faith as a true religion and philosophy.[7]

---

5. In the Septuagint, the root *apologéomai* appears only rarely (Wisd 6:11 [LXX 6:10]; 2 Macc 13:27; Jer 12:1, 20:12, 31:6 [LXX 38:6]) and mostly in connection with the Hebrew root *rîb*, a common word for "strife, controversy, dispute," in court setting as well as others. Hatch and Redpath, *Concordance to Septuagint*, 138. See Liedke, "*rîb* streiten," 771–77.

6. Louw and Nida, *Greek-English Lexicon*, 388–445 (§33.A–D).

7. Fiedrowicz, *Apologie*, 16–19, 21. Skarsaune, "Apologie II," 631–32 indicates that Eusebius of Caesarea (263–339 CE) already describes a variety of early Christian texts as apologetic literature: the apology of Quadratus (ca. 125 CE, not preserved. IV 3,1.3), the apology of Aristides (ca. 140 CE), two apologies of Justin (the first of them ca. 155 CE. IV 8,3, 11,8–12, 18,2), apologies of Melito of Sardes, Apollinaris Claudius, and Miltiades (these three about 175/6 CE, not preserved. IV 26,1, V 17,5), as well as the *Apologeticum* of Tertullian (197 CE. V 5,5). Texts of similar character (not mentioned by Eusebius) are *Legatio* by Athenagoras of Athens (ca. 175/6 CE), *Kerygma Petri* (ca. 125 CE), *Oratio ad Graecos* by Tatian, *Ad Autolycum* by Theophilus of Anitochia, *Protreptikos* by Clemens of Alexandria, *Ad Diognetum* (anonymous, date disputed), *Octavius* by Minucius Felix and the most important pseudo-Justinian exhortation epistle: *Cohortatio ad Gentiles* (third century CE?).

TOWARDS A MODERN UNDERSTANDING

Many scholars today would describe apologetics as a vindication and substantiation of faith.[8] On the other hand, Protestant theologians such as Helmuth Schreiner, Gerrit Cornelis Berkouwer, Paul Tillich, and Emil Brunner have emphasized that apologetics should not be misunderstood as a defense, but as an "answer" (Tillich) and—even stronger—*Angriff,* "offense, attack":

> The name "apologetic" is hampered by the suggestion of a *defence* of Christianity at the bar of Reason, even if it does not go so far as to claim rational *proof.* Actually, however, what matters is not "defence" but "attack"—the *attack,* namely, of the Church on the opposing positions of unbelief, superstition, or misleading ideologies.[9]

The dualism of "negative" (reactive) and "positive" (proactive) apologetics[10] alone does not seem to be able to do justice to the complete semantic range of the term. The reformed theologian

---

8. Seckler, "Apologetik I," 835. See the "classical approach" apologist Geisler and his very short definition "*Apologetics* is the discipline that deals with a rational defense of Christian faith," in Geisler, *Baker Encyclopedia of Christian Apologetics,* 37. A good example for an intentional restriction to the "negative" (defensive) task of apologetics is in Plantinga, "Self-Profile," 33: "the attempt to defend Christianity (or more broadly, theism) against the various sorts of attacks brought against it." He came to believe that a "positive" task of apologetics (establishing the truth of Christian theism) has not been crowned with success. See Mascord, *Alvin Plantinga,* 23.

9. Brunner, *Christian Doctrine of God,* 98; Schreiner, *Geist und Gestalt,* quoted in Adam, *Aufgabe,* 108; Tillich, *Systematic Theology I,* 6; Bayer, *Theologie,* 20; see "courageously ventured witness," Berkouwer, *Half Century,* 26, referring to his predecessor at the Free University Amsterdam, Valentin Hepp, quoted in Dyrness, *Christian Apologetics,* 13.

10. Use of the terms "negative" and "positive," according to Cowan, "Introduction," 8. The terms "reactive" and "proactive," according to Stackhouse, *Humble Apologetics,* 115–16; see the opposed pair "proactive" and "responsive,"

John Frame and others[11] try to combine all three aspects of apologetics, mentioned by Brunner:

- Proof
- Defense
- Offense

Many other definitions can be categorized into one of these three. The Swiss reformed scholar Heinrich Ott describes apologetics in the tradition of Barth (see below) as "rendering an account" *(Rechenschaftsablage)*, thus leading in the direction of defense. His Catholic colleague Frank Usarski, a German scholar in Brazil, talks about "validation" *(Plausibilisierung)*, therefore tending in the direction of proof.[12] In the same direction goes the Anglican priest Alan Richardson when he refers to the relationship of Christian faith to "the wider sphere of man's 'secular' knowledge," and the aim of demonstrating the truth of faith.[13] In his seminal dissertation on the task of apologetics, the German Protestant theologian Alfred Adam describes apologetics more offensively and as a "removal of obstacles to faith" *(Beseitigung von Glaubenshindernissen)*.[14] In

---

Beilby, *Thinking About Christian Apologetics*, 17.

11. Frame, *Apologetics*, 2–3. See the survey in Boa and Bowman, *Faith*, 4–7, which refer to Beattie, *Apologetics*, 56, and Ramm, *God who Makes*, 15–19 with similar three element definitions. Boa and Bowman prefer the four element definition of Reymond, *Justification of Knowledge*, 5–7, who adds the element that apologetics seeks to persuade people of the truth of the Christian position. Boa and Bowman concede that this could also be viewed as indicating the overall purpose of apologetics. Others would challenge the possibility or idea of assignment to persuade people of faith (see 2 Cor 5:11). Obviously, there are limitations to persuasion: apologetics cannot compel belief and cannot create faith. Beilby, *Thinking About Christian Apologetics*, 25–26.

12. Usarski, "Apologetik I," 661.

13. Richardson, *Christian Apologetics*, 19. See the description of the task of apologetics to lay "before the watching world such a winsome embodiment of the Christian faith that for any and all who are willing to observe there will be an intellectually and emotionally credible witness to its fundamental truth," Sire, *Little Primer*, 26.

14. Adam, *Aufgabe*, 69–70.

a similar way, the British systematic theologian Alister McGrath defines:

> Apologetics aims to identify these barriers of faith, whatever their nature, and offer responses that help to overcome them.[15]

He names three themes of apologetics: "defending," "commending," and—with reference to C.S. Lewis[16]—"translating." The aspect of offen se does not appear.

Compared to the above, the sociological definition by the Jewish scholar Robert Chazan appears to be out of the ordinary, and yet remarkable. For him the task of apologetics is "to show the superiority of the in-group vision and commitments to those of outsiders."[17]

The semantic vagueness and uncertainty of the modern understanding around apologetics makes it difficult to get a clear view of the basis of this subject within the Old Testament. However, some historical insights might help to outline a working definition of apologetics that can serve as an essential starting point for this study.

---

15. McGrath, *Mere Apologetics*, 18; See McGrath, "Evangelical Apologetics," 3–10. There are different designations for these obstacles or barriers, as Powell, *Holman QuickSource Guide*, 5 itemizes "objections, barriers, biases, acculturations, conditions, misconceptions, presuppositions, distortions of facts, and any number of excuses. It is the goal of Christian apologetics to remove these hindrances." See Carnell, *Introduction to Christian Apologetics*, 8, who wants to "remove from critics any excuse," and Ramm, *Protestant Christian Evidences*, 16, who talks about prejudice, mistaken notions, biased opinions, and objections.

16. "You must translate every bit of your theology into the vernacular," Lewis, *God in the Dock*, 96, full quote in McGrath, *Mere Apologetics*, 20. Similar to McGrath, Beilby, *Thinking About Christian Apologetics*, 14 speaks of "defending and commending the faith," but leaves out the third term.

17. Chazan, "Apologetics I," 414.

SCHLEIERMACHER'S DEFINITION OF APOLOGETICS WITHIN THE SYSTEM OF THEOLOGY

The Protestant scholar Karl Heinrich Sack (1789–1875) and the Catholic scholar Johann Sebastian von Drey (1777–1853) can be considered the fathers of modern day apologetics.[18] Both theologians distinguish their scholarly reflected "apologetics" from what had been practiced before them as an "apology" of the Christian faith.[19] Sack defines Christian apologetics as "the theological discipline dealing with the basis of Christian religion as divine matter of fact."[20] The definition of von Drey is embedded in the title of his three volume principal work, *Die Apologetik als wissenschaftliche Nachweisung der Göttlichkeit des Christenthums in seiner Erscheinung*: Directly translated this means: "Apologetics as scholarly verification of the divineness of Christianity in its appearance."[21]

Sack and von Drey both stand in the liberal tradition of Friedrich Daniel Ernst Schleiermacher (1768–1834), who defines a precise position of apologetics within the other theological disciplines in his *Brief Outline of Theology as a Field of Study* (1811, 1830).[22] Schleiermacher himself stands in the tradition of Gottlieb

---

18. See Kustermann, *Apologetik Johann*, 119–26, referring to Dulles, *History of Apologetics*, 180–81, 200.

19. Sack, *Christliche Apologetik*, 20–21; von Drey, *Apologetik als wissenschaftlich*, 17–19.

20. "Die christliche Apologetik ist die theologische Disziplin von dem Grunde der christlichen Religion als einer göttlichen Thatsache," Sack, *Christliche Apologetik*, 1, my translation.

21. My translation. See Kustermann, *Apologetik Johann*, 236. Quite similar, Warfield, "Apologetics," 234: "the science which establishes the truth of Christianity as the absolute religion."

22. Schleiermacher, *Brief Outline*; German edition: *Kurze Darstellung*. This work summarizes his lectures "Theologische Enzyklopädie," which he taught in the years 1804–1832 in Halle and Berlin. See Schleiermacher, *Theologische Enzyklopädie*, and as an introduction, Birkner, "Schleiermachers 'Kurze Darstellung,'" 285–305; Rössler, *Schleiermachers Programm*, 215–20. Schleiermacher himself follows his scheme only marginally in four "propositions" *(Lehnsätzen)* in his introduction to *Christian Faith*, 52–76 [§11–14].

Jakob Planck (1751–1833), who was the first to conduct a classification of apologetics as a theological discipline.[23]

For Schleiermacher, *apologetics* (with a "wholly outward" direction) has to be distinguished from *polemics* (with a "wholly inward" direction, against deviation in doctrine within the Christian community).[24] Both—apologetics and polemics—are part of "philosophical theology," which is put in front of all the other disciplines of theology, which can in turn be divided into the categories "historical theology" and "practical theology":

> Accordingly, historical theology is the actual corpus of theological study, which corpus is interconnected with science, as such, by means of philosophical theology and is interconnected with the active Christian life by means of practical theology.[25]

With this arrangement, apologetics serves as the entrance and basis of Schleiermacher's theological system:

---

23. His definition of apologetics is still quite different to the definition of Schleiermacher: "Man hat zwar diesen Nahmen erst neuerlich, ja erst zu unserer Zeit für die Kenntnis und Wissenschaft derjenigen Beweise erfunden, durch welche die Göttlichkeit des Christenthums, oder das göttliche Ansehen und der göttliche Ursprung der christlichen Lehre gegen Einwürfe aller Art behauptet und gerettet werden kann," Planck, *Einleitung in die Theologische*, 303. Steck, "Apologetik II," 416.

24. Schleiermacher, *Brief Outline*, 20 [§41].

25. Schleiermacher, *Christian Faith*, 13 [§28].

THE ACTIVE CHRISTIAN LIFE
↑ *connected to* ↑

PRACTICAL THEOLOGY
Church Service | Church Government

HISTORICAL THEOLOGY
Exegetical Theology | Church History | Dogmatic Theology | Church Statistics

PHILSOPHICAL THEOLOGY
Apologetics | Polemics

↓ *connected to* ↓
SCIENCE

The Three-Part Organization of Theological Studies according to Friedrich Daniel Ernst Schleiermacher's *Brief Outline of Theology as a Field of Study* **(1811, 1830)**

The "basic task" of apologetics according to Schleiermacher is to point out "the distinctive nature of Christianity" *(das eigenthümliche Wesen des Christenthums)* in "relation to the special character of other religious communities."[26] One could describe Schleiermacher's agenda of apologetics as a comparative theory of religion with a special focus on Christianity[27] and a basic conviction that "Christianity is, in fact, the most perfect and of the most highly developed forms of religion."[28]

The aim of apologetics is not to be commingled with practical concerns: "By this use of the term 'apologetics' no other defense

26. Schleiermacher, *Brief Outline*, 21 [§44].
27. Nowak, *Schleiermacher*, 226.
28. Schleiermacher, *Christian Faith*, 38 [§8]. Referring to both the superiority of Christianity to other religions and their juxtaposition, Barth, *Protestant Theology*, 430 observes in Schleiermacher a "bolder and a more cautious approach to the apologetic task." See Forstmann, "Barth, Schleiermacher," 310–15.

is meant than that which seeks to ward off hostility towards the community. The endeavor to bring others into this community is a clerical practice," and thus has to be situated within the division of Practical Theology.[29]

Schleiermacher summarizes the content of Christian apologetics by mentioning and explaining the following concepts:

- "revelation," "miracle," and "inspiration"
- "prophecy" and "model" (*Vorbild*)
- "canon" and "sacrament"
- "hierarchy" and "church authority"[30]

Apologetics has to be strictly distinguished from polemics, which is directed towards "diseased deviations arising in the community to which one belongs,"[31] and not "outwardly, for example against the Catholics, or . . . the Jews or even against deists and atheists."[32]

BARTH'S CHALLENGE TO THE LEGITIMACY OF APOLOGETICS AS AUTONOMOUS DISCIPLINE

In his lectures on *Protestant Theology in the Nineteenth Century* (first printed 1947),[33] Karl Barth (1886–1968) provides a lengthy definition of apologetics in discussion with Schleiermacher, where he makes a distinction between a bold approach (trying to prove the necessity of Christian truth) and a more cautious approach (trying to prove its possibility):

> Apologetics is an attempt to show by means of thought and speech that the determining principle of philosophy and of historical and natural research at some given point in time certainly do not preclude, even if they do

29. Schleiermacher, *Brief Outline*, 20 [§39].
30. Schleiermacher, *Brief Outline*, 21–22 [§45–48].
31. Schleiermacher, *Brief Outline*, 19 [§40].
32. Schleiermacher, *Brief Outline*, 20 [§41].
33. Barth, *Protestantische Theologie*.

What Do We Understand by Apologetics?

not directly require the tenets of theology, which are founded upon revelation and upon faith respectively. A bold apologetics proves to a particular generation the intellectual necessity of the theological principles taken from the Bible or from church dogma or from both; a more cautious apologetics proves at least their intellectual possibility. About the extent and content of these principles opinions may of course vary among the apologists themselves, and within the same period of time.[34]

A shorter definition can be found in his voluminous *Church Dogmatics*, where Barth sums up the task of apologetics as "to give ... account" *Rechenschaftsablage*:

> [to] prepare an exact account of the presupposition, limits, meaning and basis of the statements of the Christian confession, and thus be able to give this account to any who may demand it.[35]

After having defined what he means by apologetics, Karl Barth not only questions the place of apologetics in Schleiermacher's theological system, but the total idea of it.

We see this in Barth's dispute with his contemporary Emil Brunner, who demands an "eristic"[36] prolegomena to dogmatics,[37] i.e., a theological "foreword," arguing for the warrant of what follows. Barth now envisions the theologian who intends to start writing his dogmatic work. However, before he can write the first letter, he has to "drop" the given task (one could imagine how he

---

34. Barth, *Protestant Theology*, 425–26.
35. Barth, *Church Dogmatics*, IV, 3.2, 109 [§69]. More precisely, in German: "eine genaue Rechenschaftsablage über die Voraussetzungen, über die Grenze, über den Sinn und über den Grund der Sätze des christlichen Bekenntnisses," Barth, *Kirchliche Dogmatik*, 121. See Steck, "Apologetik II," 411.
36. The term "eristic" (from *Eris*, the Greek goddess of strife) is used in this context as alternative to "apologetic."
37. Barth, *Church Dogmatics*, 27 [§2] explicitly refers to Brunner, "Die andere Aufgabe," 255–76.

drops his pen) "at once,"³⁸ and is distracted by a side track issue. This amounts to an "abandonment rather than the serious acceptance" of his task:

> the sphere of the Church is abandoned and "another task" is indeed substituted for the task of dogmatics. . . . prolegomena to dogmatics do not so much lead up to the real work of dogmatics as lead away from it.³⁹

Barth rejects the concept of apologetics as independent discipline (separated from or, outside of, dogmatics) for three reasons, which derive from his distinct approach to theology:⁴⁰ (a) Apologetics would "take unbelief seriously," contradicting his idea of faith. (b) It would appear that there is not enough work to be done in dogmatics itself. (c) Dogmatics would run the risk of thinking that there is no more conflict with disbelief. However, the opposite is true; according to Barth, apologetics is not a prelude to dogmatics—dogmatics has to be apologetic as a whole. "At every point, therefore, dogmatics is a struggle between this reason of man and the revelation believed in the Church."⁴¹

Barth's one-sided rejection of "autonomous" apologetics can be understood on the background of the previously mentioned dispute with Emil Brunner. However, his arguments are unconvincing for many after him. Even he himself accepts prolegomena in the end, although they should not be grounded in a conflict with unbelief, but evolve out of "inner necessity grounded in the matter itself."⁴² Furthermore, prolegomena to dogmatics are possible only as part of dogmatics itself. "The prefix *pro* in prolegomena is to be understood loosely to signify the first part of dogmatics rather than that which is prior to it."⁴³

---

38. Unfortunately the English translation does not express the picturesque language: "mit der die Aufgabe der Dogmatik sofort fallen gelassen statt in Angriff genommen wird," Barth, *Kirchliche Dogmatik*, 1, 28 [§2].

39. Barth, *Church Dogmatics*, 28–29 [§2].

40. Barth, *Church Dogmatics*, 30.

41. Barth, *Church Dogmatics*, 28–29.

42. Barth, *Church Dogmatics*, 31.

43. Barth, *Church Dogmatics*, 42.

CONSEQUENCES

Barth's radical challenge of apologetics indeed opens the way for further questions concerning the concept of Schleiermacher:

1. If one accepts Barth's definition of apologetics, the inner logic of Schleiermacher's organization of theological studies can no longer be safeguarded against serious criticism. How can one defend the "theological principles taken from the Bible or from church dogma or from both"—how can one give an "exact account" of the statements of the Christian confession, if they are not yet developed?

In a way, one could say that Barth turns away from Schleiermacher's double function of apologetics. Apologetics is no longer understood as a philosophy of religion *and* defense ("to ward off hostility"), but only as defense that is fed from philosophy of religion.[44] Therefore, it becomes logically possible to relocate the position of apologetics.

On the basis of a concept of apologetics similar to that of Barth, Alfred Adam argues for the necessity to understand apologetics as "a transition from dogmatics to practical theology":[45]

> if [dogmatics] has not already developed its material, apologetics is left without a distinct point of origin and without a distinct and determined aim as regards to content. Only after dogmatics has spoken can apologetics arise.[46]

Without dogmatics, apologetics has neither substance, mandate, nor meaning. Therefore, many would conclude to move apologetics from the "entrance" to the "exit" of dogmatics.

---

44. See Adam, *Aufgabe*, 123–24.

45. Jelke, "Aufgabe der Dogmatik," 42, quoted in Adam, *Aufgabe*, 12, my translation. See Adam, *Aufgabe*, 49.

46. Adam, *Aufgabe*, 52, my translation. See Lemme, "Apologetik, Apologie," 682–83.

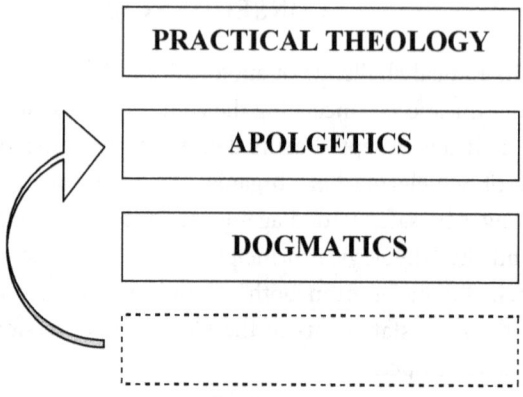

Rearrangement of Schleiermacher's system
according to Alfred Adam, *Die Aufgabe der Apologetik* (1931)

2. With his outright rejection of eristic prolegomena, Barth has shown that there is more to "philosophical theology" than apologetics and polemics. It has not proven viable to restrict the matter of prolegomena in the way Schleiermacher did.

We can observe this conceptual uncertainty since the end of the nineteenth century, where the terms "apologetics" and "fundamental theology" oftentimes were used—especially by Catholic theologians—in a virtually synonymous way. The Catholic scholar Max Seckler points out that for the sake of precision it seems to make much more sense to distinguish clearly between these two concepts:

- Fundamental theology stands at the beginning and has the task of "self-determination" of the fundamental and foundational elements of Christian theology.

- Apologetics stands at the end and has the task of "self-assertion," the perpetuation of Christian truth to the outside.[47]

---

47. Seckler, "Apologetik IV," 840, talks about Selbsterfassung (Ermittlung) and Selbstbehauptung. See Verweyen, *Einführung*, 46–47; Ott, *Apologetik*, 9–13; Seckler, "Apologetik I," 835; Wagner, "Apologetik V," 844.

Regardless of whether one concurs with Barth on the determination to *include* prolegomena into dogmatics ("on its way, and then on this way, admittedly perhaps as its first task"), or follows the (according to Barth) "Modernist and Roman Catholic" way of setting them apart "before actually embarking on dogmatics"[48]—many Protestant and Catholic scholars would agree today that there is the need for prolegomena and that these prolegomena have to be distinguished from what is defined as apologetics:

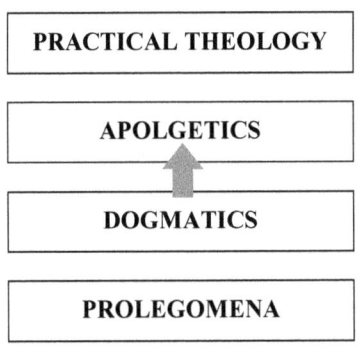

3. When Schleiermacher defines apologetics as a part of "philosophical theology," he is forced to separate the theoretical part of apologetics ("principles") from its practical part ("technology"). He admits that the later "would make up the division of practical theology that rests directly upon apologetics."[49] However, this separation can hardly be justified only on the basis of conceptual presumptions.[50] Even though both parts can be clearly distinguished methodologically, they nevertheless stay inseparably connected.

There is an analogy between the relationship of the theoretical to the practical part of apologetics on the one hand and the

48. Barth, *Church Dogmatics I*, 42 [§2].

49. Schleiermacher, *Brief Outline*, 19, uses the term "principles" only in relation to polemics [§40], nevertheless, it is implied in the distinction made in §39 as well (all on same page).

50. See the criticism of Aland, *Apologie*, 14. When Schleiermacher describes the function of apologetics virtually as philosophy of religion, Aland misses the for-him essential practical function of apologetics: "auf die zweite, den praktischen Gebrauch, muß es ihr ankommen."

relationship of dogmatics to homiletics on the other. Homiletics as the art of preaching is based on dogmatics as the provider of substance and content. In a similar way, the practical part of apologetics as the art of defense is based on the theoretical part as its provider. Content and method—the "what" and the "how"—come together within the discipline of apologetics.[51]

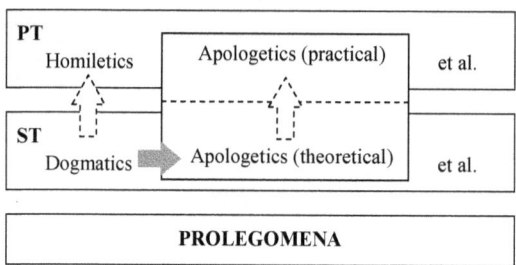

The arrangement of *theoretical* and *practical apologetics* parallel to *dogmatics* and *homiletics* within the disciplines of *Practical* and *Systematic Theology* according to Max Seckler (1993)

4. There are further points of criticism on Schleiermacher, which can not be treated here extensively. Even though he assumes a superiority of Christianity, his philosophical approach, which starts with the comparison of "communities of faith," relativizes the absoluteness claim of Christian faith from the outset. Furthermore, one can observe in Schleiermacher a subordination of theology under the realm of philosophy in the claim that the outset of "philosophical theology" has to be taken "above" Christianity.[52] The observable demise of liberal apologetics in the academic world could be interpreted as the result of these decisions.

As we will see in this further investigation, from a biblical-theological standpoint, the God of the Hebrews does not avoid being compared with other deities. However, this comparison

---

51. Seckler, "Apologetik I," 836; See Zöckler, *Geschichte der Apologie*, 5–6; Adam, *Aufgabe*, 91–103; Beißer, "Grundlegung," 210.

52. Both statements can be found in Schleiermacher, *Brief Outline*, 15 [§33]. Criticism of both by Adam, *Aufgabe*, 20.

only exposes his incomparability—he is alive, they are dead. This indicates an intrinsic tension between the core of biblical theology and the graduated view of Schleiermacher.

It has been questioned if Schleiermacher really could do justice to the liveliness of God, his reactions to human behavior and his sovereignty, which cannot be captured in the nets of our small, controllable human ideas. For Schleiermacher these descriptions of "God" are all expressions of human religious experience.[53] Blaise Pascal (1623–1662), one of the greatest apologists of all time and died far too young, gave testimony to this tension in his own personal way long before Schleiermacher's days. On a *mémorial*, a small piece of parchment, sewn into his coat, Pascal reminds himself of the day he came to know the living God and makes a clear distinction when he writes: "God of Abraham, God of Isaac, God of Jacob, not of the philosophers and savants." As long as we are able to subsume our reflection on "God" below the discipline of philosophy, it is questionable how well we really understand who God is.

WORKING DEFINITION AND DEMARCATIONS

On the basis of the above made differentiations, it is possible to contour the idea of apologetics by the following working definition:

> Apologetics is the dispute of Christian truth with (1) extrinsic, (2) contemporary truth claims, (3) while accounting for content and method. (4) Furthermore, apologetics operations defensively and offensively, and thereby referring to one's own system and to the opponent's.

In detail:

1. Whereas "polemics" deals with deviations within one's own community according to Schleiermacher (e.g., Protestant

---

53. Leiner, *Methodischer Leitfaden*, 25–27, referring to the criticism by Brunner, *Mystik und Wort*.

versus Catholic within the Christian church), apologetics is always directed to the outside.[54]

2. Whereas dogmatics deals with problems within one's own doctrine, apologetics sets Christian truth in relation to foreign, contemporary claims of truth.[55]

3. The discipline of apologetics can be subdivided in two parts: in its original doctrinal-substantiating function, apologetics is connected to the discipline of Systematic Theology. Its rhetoric-cultural function can be assigned to the discipline of Practical Theology. The first aspect reflects on content, the second on the method of the practice of apologetics, the "art" of defense. Apologetics as a whole brings together content and method.

4. The etymology of apologetics does not lead to a restriction to the meaning of defense. Oftentimes, the aspect of offense and attack is emphasized. This implies that the realm of dispute is not confined to the Christian faith. Rather a "dispute about the truth of what is believed on both sides" is explicitly included.[56] The apologist has to be able to think his way into other belief systems and evaluate arguments in favor of the meaningfulness of their paradigm with those against it.

---

54. Beilby, *Thinking About Christian Apologetics*, 20 describes this restriction from another perspective: "The proper domain of apologetics is the defense of dogma, not doctrines." According to his definition, dogmas are "core Christian claims," whereas doctrines deal with their explanation and application (p. 19). Therefore, apologetics is not about doctrinal disputes between Christians.

55. Adam, *Aufgabe*, 121. See Steck, "Apologetik II," 420, referring to the issue of a clear distinction between dogmatics and apologetics.

56. "Streit um die Wahrheit des auf beiden Seiten Geglaubten," Beißer, *Der christliche Glaube 1*, 108, my translation. See Beilby, *Thinking About Christian Apologetics*, 17 with the definition of "'deconstructive arguments" ("arguments against the truthfulness of other worldviews") and "undercutting arguments" ("responses to an objection designed to show that the objection itself is misguided"). He opposes deconstructive to constructive arguments (both in the category of "proactive apologetics") and undercutting to rebutting arguments (both in the category of "responsive apologetics").

2

Apologetics and Biblical Theology

TERMINOLOGICAL CLARIFICATIONS IN RELATION TO BIBLICAL STUDIES

As WE HAVE SEEN, Karl Heinrich Sack and Johann Sebastian von Drey differentiated between their academic, methodologically reflected "apologetics" and (from their perspective) the more simple attempts of "apology" before them.

For others, "apologetics" denotes the overall system of defense, while "apology" only describes the individual act "from case to case, each in individual situations, depending on the particular attacks."[1]

A third way is to distinguish "apologetics" as pure methodological study from "apology" as the practice of defense. However, it has been found difficult to keep these two areas separated.[2]

These three differentiations have also been used in a partly overlapping way. However, none of them have become established amongst scholars of biblical interpretation. With regard to the New Testament, a fourth approach has been suggested. Here, one usually distinguishes between "apology" as literary genre and

---

1. Beißer, "Grundlegung," 211, 213.
2. Aland, *Apologie*, 15. See Adam, *Aufgabe*, 69. Zöckler, *Geschichte*, 4–5.

"apologetics" as the method of argumentation.[3] So we end up with at least[4] four different ways of relating these two terms to each other:

	'Apologetics'	*'Apology'*
Modern Theology (Sack/ von Drey)	methodologically reflected approach	methodologically not/less reflected
Modern Theology (alternative)	overall system	treatment of individual topics
Modern Theology (alternative)	methodological study	practice of defense
New Testament Studies	method of theological argumentation	literary genre

According to Klaus Berger, the genre of "apology" can be found with the defense speeches of Paul in Acts 23:1–6, 24:10–21, 25:8, 26:2–23, and possibly 22:1–21.[5] Here, apology denotes a self-defense speech in court, which has to be distinguished from the defense of a third party, e.g., God. Even though he is giving testimony to his faith, Paul is speaking for himself in defense:

> Agrippa said to Paul, "You have permission to speak for yourself *[perí seautoú légein]*." Then Paul stretched out his hand and began to defend himself *[apelogeíto]*: "I consider myself fortunate that it is before you, King Agrippa, I am to make my defense *[apologeísthai]* today

---

3. Guerra, "Romans 4," 252–53. See Guerra, *Romans*, 2–3; Neagoe, *Trial of the Gospel*, 5, n. 9.

4. See Richardson, *Christian Apologetics*, 20: "apologetics is primarily a study undertaken by Christians for Christians; and in this respect it is to be distinguished from the task of apology, since an apology is addressed to non-Christians." Further attempts to distinguish apologetics from apology in Bahnsen, "Socrates or Christ," 191, quoted Boa and Bowman, *Faith*, 3.

5. In addition, Matt 7:22–23, 27:24; Luke 13:26–27; and Acts 4:7–12, 5:28–32.

against all the accusations *[egkaloúmai]* of the Jews, ..."
(Acts 26:1-2).⁶

Apologies in a broader sense can be found in Romans 9 and 11. Also, the Gospel of John and the second letter to the Corinthians can be understood as apologies from a literary perspective.⁷

In the realm of Old Testament studies, one hardly encounters such terms as "apologetics" or "apology." Instead the term "polemics" is preferred. It is used in a broad sense for the confrontation between various ideological positions, primarily within the Bible.⁸ The term is used here in a fundamentally different way than it was used by Friedrich Schleiermacher, who saw the essence of "polemics" in the aspect of inner-religious orientation.⁹ In Old Testament scholarship (as well as in colloquial language), the aspect of attack and confrontation is in view, without excluding the aspects of stabilization and defense of one's own faith. This usage corresponds to the understanding of "polemics" in the discipline of religious studies, where one can differentiate between *intra-faith, inter-faith,* and *extra-faith polemics*.¹⁰ According to this terminology, Schleiermacher's "polemics" would always be narrowed down to *intra-faith polemics,* directed only against deviations within one's own community of faith. However, in biblical and religious studies, we have a much broader view. Without changing the working definition of apologetics as being directed only to the outside, we will however

---

6. See *mou apologías,* "my apology," in Acts 22:1, *tá perí emautoú apologoúmai,* "make my defense," in 24:10, and *autoú apologouménou,* "his defense," in 26:24.

7. Further examples in Berger, *Formen und Gattungen,* 425-28, as well as Berger, *Formgeschichte,* 360-63; See the classification as "forensic speech" in Winter, "Official Proceedings," 305-36.

8. Amit, *Hidden Polemics,* 3-24.

9. Schleiermacher, *Brief Outline,* 20 [§41], was already aware by himself that his definition deviated from "the far more common usage of the term," which at his time was a "clerical practice in the broader sense of the term." See the evaluation of Hettema, "Noble Art," 27, who doubts "whether the act of polemicizing is fully described by Schleiermacher's theory."

10. Dascal, "Uses of Argumentative Reason," 9-17.

use the term "polemics" in the following chapters in the broader sense rather than the limited way of Schleiermacher.

Outward Direction (inter-/extra-faith polemics)	*Inward Direction* (intra-faith polemics)
Apologetics	**'Polemics'** (Schleiermacher)
'Polemics' (Old Testament Studies, Religious Studies, colloquially)	

There are a number of Old Testament studies particularly on the phenomenon of "cult polemic,"[11] which is polemics directed against religious tendencies within the Israelite community, especially against the religious practice of the Jerusalem cult. However, these studies can only partly contribute to a biblical theology of apologetics. Outwardly directed "polemics," in the actual sense of "'apologetics," can also be found in the Old Testament, which confronts the religious culture of the surrounding nations, particularly against their worship of idols. (In how far those messages were historically received by the foreign nations is another question. Jonah is certainly one example that they were).[12]

Since foreign religious practices also occur within the ethnically defined society of Israel, the boundaries between internal and external are blurred. Referring to such pluralistic (some would say "syncretistic") phenomena within one religion, Günther Lanczkowski has coined the term "religious internal pluralism."[13] In the

---

11. Concerning the state of research on cult polemic texts: von Knorre, *Vergeblicher Gottesdienst*, 16–53 and, furthermore, Snoek, "Religious Polemics," 507–88.

12. The observation made by Schultz, "'Und sie verkünden,'" 45, "Wir haben keine konkreten Hinweise, daß diese Botschaften je an die Nationen 'abgeschickt' wurden. (Jonas Zwangsbesuch in Ninive ist kein ausreichender Beweis dafür)," referring to Isa 13–23, Jer 46–51, Amos 1–2, Zeph 2:4–15.

13. "Religionsinterner Pluralismus," Lanczkowski, *Begegnung und Wandel*, 50–55, taken up in Old Testament studies by Rose, *Ausschließlichkeitsanspruch Jahwes*, and Albertz, *Persönliche Frömmigkeit*.

Old Testament, there are examples of Israelite prophets who actually encouraged apostasy from YHWH, as announced in the book of Deuteronomy:

> If prophets or those who divine by dreams appear among you and promise you omens or portents, ² and the omens or the portents declared by them take place, and they say, "Let us follow other gods" (whom you have not known) "and let us serve them," ³ you must not heed the words of those prophets or those who divine by dreams; for the LORD your God is testing you, to know whether you indeed love the LORD your God with all your heart and soul. ⁴ The LORD your God you shall follow, him alone you shall fear, his commandments you shall keep, his voice you shall obey, him you shall serve, and to him you shall hold fast. ⁵ But those prophets or those who divine by dreams shall be put to death for having spoken treason against the LORD your God—who brought you out of the land of Egypt and redeemed you from the house of slavery—to turn you from the way in which the LORD your God commanded you to walk. So you shall purge the evil from your midst (Deut 13:1–5).

From an ethnic perspective, this course of action (the killing of the false prophets) is directed toward the inside, against the Israelite people. From a religious perspective of Deuteronomic theology, it is directed toward the outside, against foreign religion.

Therefore, a biblical theology of Old Testament apologetics must also respect such cases of polemics that concern the existential foundation of the religious community, especially where its loyalty to YHWH appears to be fundamentally endangered.

PRELIMINARY METHODOLOGICAL CONSIDERATIONS WITHIN BIBLICAL THEOLOGY

In contrast to a history of Israelite religion, biblical theology does not aim to reconstruct the historical development of Old Testament beliefs, but to present a "synopsis of the Old Testament world of belief and testimony."[14] Traditionally, scholars ordered this synopsis according to the history of the Bible's composition that they accepted (diachronically). In recent times however, scholars such as Brevard Childs and Rolf Rendtorff have attempted to expose the advantages of a synchronic, literary-canonical reading of the biblical texts.[15] Such a synchronic investigation follows the canonical order of texts, themes and books. It orients itself directly by the biblical presentation of events—their ordering and interconnectedness—"as the faith of Israel saw them."[16]

The thematic scope of a canonical investigation must not be narrowed down by theological concepts that have been developed outside of the canon, but finds its subject matter within the texts themselves. This means that the modern concept of "apologetics" does not function as an organizing principle or lead to theological restrictions. It can only serve as a kind of overarching field of themes, hinting at the way to relevant evidence within the biblical texts. From the outset, we have to be open to the possibility that not only one, but several concepts may appear within the framework of our investigation, which may not inevitably be brought into relation with one another. According to a multiplex-canonical approach, such concepts will be followed with a longitudinal perspective throughout the biblical texts. Only at the end of the investigation can we ask for an inner unity of the theme-lines, connecting the divergent themes and concepts on a deeper level.[17]

FORMS OF APOLOGETIC STRATEGY IN THE OLD TESTAMENT

The only work that has ever specifically intended to outline an Old Testament theology of apologetics was written in 1958 by

14. "eine Zusammenschau der Glaubens- und Zeugniswelt des AT," Preuß, *Theologie 1*, 1–2; See Rendtorff, "Hermeneutik einer kanonischen," 36–39.

15. Childs, *Biblical Theology*; Rendtorff, *Theologie 1*; See Koorevaar and Paul, *Theologie van het Oude Testament*.

16. von Rad, *Old Testament Theology*, 120, translation of *Theologie I*, 134.

17. Hasel, *Old Testament Theology*, 203–6.

the Baptist apologist Bernard Ramm (1916–1992). In his six page article, written for an evangelical journal, he concentrates on the prophetic books (the "latter prophets" in Jewish terminology), especially Jeremiah. Focusing on the *subject matter*, he detects a single-tracked theme line: The core of Old Testament apologetics is about the living God and his distinction from the dead idols. This is not so much a question of true or false, nor of existent or non-existent, but of living and dead. According to Ramm, the Old Testament elaborates this distinction through the following "media":

- Nature
- History
- The quality of God's self-manifestation
- The futility of his opponents[18]

Ramm's article did not receive much attention, probably because it overlapped thematically with the question of polemics against foreign gods and idols, which had been already dealt with extensively in his time. However, Ramm has to be given credit for highlighting the value of these theological results for the discipline of Christian apologetics.

A broader investigation of all parts of the Hebrew canon reveals that the diversity of Old Testament apologetics only becomes evident when more attention is paid to the aspects of their *formal* presentation. Yairah Amit distinguishes between three types of Old Testament polemics:

- Explicit polemics
- Implicit polemics (the theme is explicitly mentioned, but referred to only in an indirect way)
- Hidden polemics (the theme is not mentioned, not explicitly mentioned, or mentioned, but not in an expected way)

---

18. Ramm, "Apologetic," 15–20.

It is precisely the two non-explicit types of polemics that seem to be strikingly effective:

> In order to determine the outcome, it was necessary to employ different types of offensive including open polemic as well as hidden polemic. The advantage of the latter lies precisely in its indirect approach, which at times succeeds more easily in convincing.[19]

These observations enlarge the view beyond the explicit polemics of the biblical prophets. However, on closer reading it becomes evident that the individual parts of the canon develop quite diversified forms of indirect and hidden polemic.

In his broadly based theological study on the apologetic theme "mockery of foreign religions in the Old Testament" *(Verspottung fremder Religionen im Alten Testament),* Horst Dietrich Preuß develops a three part survey of the investigated texts according to *literary genres.* Here, he distinguishes between mocking religion polemics that are found in narrative texts, in prophetic texts and in poetry. In the wisdom literature he does not find any record of this kind of polemic.[20] Preuß makes a convincing case in presenting a literarily determined arrangement of his material. However, his genres provide a rather inflexible pattern, which can hardly do justice to possible peculiarities and emphases of the individual texts.

A *canonically* guided outline however has the potential of equally respecting aspects of content, form and literary genre. The Hebrew canon can traditionally be subdivided into three parts:

- *Torah*
  (Gen–Deut)

- *Neviim,* "Prophets":
  (*Former Prophets:* Josh–2, Kgs,
  Latter Prophets: Jer, Ezek, Isa, the twelve minor prophets)

---

19. Amit, "Hidden Polemic," 18; See Amit, *Hidden Polemics,* 57, 93, straightening the difference between implicit and hidden polemic.

20. Preuß, *Verspottung,* 269–73.

- *Ketuvim*, "Writings":
  (Ruth, Ps, Job, Prov, Eccl, Song,
  Lam, Dan, Esth, Ezra–Neh, Chr).[21]

In two recent articles, the Dutch scholar Hendrik Koorevaar defends a structural canonical "Exile and Return Model" as an alternative to the traditional "Torah Model." It has long been observed that, from a literary perspective, the intersection between Torah and Former Prophets is only secondary compared to the intersection between Former and Latter Prophets. Koorevaar supports this observation with theological arguments and suggests maintaining the order of the books, but to view them as three theologically determined blocks:

- Priest Canon
  (Genesis–Kings)
- Prophet Canon
  (Jeremiah–Malachi)
- Wisdom Canon
  (Ruth–Chronicles)[22]

Koorevaar points out a correspondence of the theological emphases of these blocks to the "offices of the three bearers of authority":[23]

- *kohēn* ('priest')
- *nabî'* ('prophet')
- *ḥāḵām* ('wise')

---

21. This order goes back to a Baraita in the Talmud tract *Baba Bathra* 14b; see text and charts "The Three Sections" and "The Earliest Jewish Orders" in Beckwith, *Old Testament Canon*, 122, 157, 206–7; text and chart "Early Canonical Lists" in Lim, *Formation of Jewish Canon*, 36, 191–92 with translation adapted from Leiman, *Canonization of Hebrew Scripture*, 52. See Brandt, *Endgestalten des Kanons*, 63.

22. Koorevaar, "Exile and Return Model," 503, 512; See Koorevaar, "Torah Model," 64–80.

23. Koorevaar, "Exile and Return Model," 504, n. 13, referring to Steinberg, *Ketuvim*, 463–84.

These three offices are mentioned together in the book of Jeremiah: "for instruction shall not perish from the priest, nor counsel from the wise, nor the word from the prophet" (Jer 18:18).[24]

Theologically, the first canon part can be described as Torah (Genesis–Deuteronomy) and "Demonstrated Torah" (Joshua–Kings).[25] From a literary perspective, this part primarily appears as narrative, since the legal material always stays embedded in the narrative framework.[26] However, "Torah" is a much broader idea than just "law" or legal material. It is to be understood as "instruction," and this can be found in the narrative material of Genesis and Exodus as well as in the laws of Leviticus and Deuteronomy:

> Genesis of course is full of instruction, about the nature of God, the history of the world and Israel. It is also instructive in giving examples of behaviour that should be imitated and mistakes that should be avoided. The same is true of the early chapters of Exodus, which demonstrate the folly of the greatest of earthly kings pitting himself against almighty God. Likewise Israel's mistakes in the wilderness are surely recorded, to remind them both of God's mercies in the past and of the danger of making the same mistakes again in the future.[27]

The second canon part is essentially prophetic. The third part presents the perspective of the wise and the scribes.

The following investigation will demonstrate that these canonically based classifications can be related to our subject. In this way, it is possible to generally distinguish between three types of apologetics:

- Narrative (instructive) apologetics
- Prophetic apologetics
- Wisdom apologetics

---

24. See Ezek 7:26, where the third office is that of the "elders," and the background in Deut 16:18–18:22, where we read about "judges and officials."

25. Koorevaar, "Exile and Return Model," 503.

26. See Sailhamer, *Pentateuch as Narrative*, 25, 33; Alexander, *From Paradise*, 114.

27. Wenham, *Exploring Old Testament*, 4.

On closer inspection, however, it becomes evident that even these three aspects together are not entirely able to do justice to the broad spectrum of theological ideas displayed in the biblical texts. Therefore, two peculiarities have to bear additional consideration:

- Citatory apologetics (as a special case of prophetic apologetics)
- Exemplary apologetics (as a special case of narrative apologetics)

These five types of apologetics are not just literary genres, but should be understood as a classification system of apologetic strategies. The types are defined not only by one certain aspect, but by form, content, *and* method. What they have in common is that they are canonically based, which means they are derived from the presentation of the subject by the canon itself.

Before the contours of these five types of apologetic strategy within the Old Testament can be outlined, we must first deal with the special status of Genesis 1:1–2:3, the most prominent but also the most disputed case of (alleged) Old Testament polemics.

3

Genesis 1:1–2:3
Between Polemics and Apologetics

WHEN THE BIBLE INTRODUCES the person of God, it does so neither in a defending nor in an obeisant way, as we would expect in comparison with other holy books of world literature. The existence of God is simply presupposed as fact. "The existence of God is a challenge and not a question." It is not God who must prove himself, but man without God. When God is ignored, it is the *person's* life that is called into question.

Not everyone would agree to this pointed interpretation of the beginning of the book of Genesis,[1] which already adumbrates the challenges associated with the identification of indirectly formulated apologetics: the quest for implicit and hidden clues always bears a high potential of controversial results. The undeniable relationship between the creation account in Genesis 1:1–2:3 and the myths of surrounding cultures has been an especially hot topic of discussion. What motivates an ancient author to refer to the origination narratives of other cultures in such an obvious way? In how far can we talk about agreement or disagreement, about acceptance or rejection, about absorption or defense?

---

1. Following Dyrness, *Themes*, 37.

GENESIS 1:1–2:3 BETWEEN POLEMICS AND APOLOGETICS

The style of the creation account can be described as prose with some poetic elements (particularly Gen 1:26–28). Since a plot is missing, the category "narrative" *(Erzählung)* is not really fitting.[2] Rather, the text is best understood as "didactic report" *(lehrhafter[3] Bericht)*.[4] The obvious parallels[5] between Gen 1:31–2:3 and the building reports of the tabernacle (Exod 39:32–43) and Solomon's temple (1 Kgs 6:38, 7:51) indicate that the account might have been understood as sort of "construction report" of the world.

SUGGESTED POLEMICS IN GENESIS 1:1–2:3

According to Gerhard von Rad in his commentary on the book of Genesis, Genesis 1:14–19, in particular, "has a strong antimythical feeling.... The expression 'lights' or 'lamps' is meant to be prosaic and degrading."[6] Horst-Dietrich Preuß even talks about "depotentiating mockery" and identifies an "antibabylonian, scoffing polemics which wants to comfort" the Hebrew reader.[7]

The above-mentioned implicit attack on the astral deities (sun, moon, stars) is not the only argument here. Many further

---

2. Hilbrands, "Zehn Thesen," 8, sums up the discussion in Coats, *Genesis*, 35–36, 41–48, 319; Ruppert, "'Urgeschichte,'" 19–32 and Ruppert, *Genesis 1*, 60.

3. von Rad, *Old Testament Theology*, 140, German term in *Theologie I*, 153.

4. For the current state of research on the discussion about "report of God's word" and "report of God's deed" *(Wort—und Tatbericht)*, Bührer, *Am Anfang*, 40–48.

5. This argument is valid irrespective of the assumed direction of literary dependency. The formal similarity has been observed in many cases; see Blenkinsopp, "Structure of P," 280, and with further references Blum, *Studien zur Komposition*, 306, n. 73, as well as Janowski, *Sühne als Heilsgeschehen*, 309–12, 445–46.

6. von Rad, *Genesis*, 55, translation of *Das erste Buch Mose*, 42.

7. Preuß, *Verspottung*, 183. More recently, Jonker, "Religious Polemics," 235–54.

obviously intended contrasts to the myths of the surrounding cultures have been identified:[8]

1. The term *təhôm* "deep" (Gen 1:2) is an intentional reference to Tiamat, a primordial goddess of the ocean.[9]
2. The sea monsters (Gen 1:21) are not rivals of God, but harmless sea animals.
3. The creation of heaven and earth as an act of separation does not originate in a conflict between gods, but by a simple divine *fiat*.
4. People are not created for the purpose of serving and providing for the gods, rather they are the climax of creation. God is the one who provides for them.
5. God creates by using his plain word, not by using magic spells.
6. The earth has to be first provided with the ability to generate food.[10]
7. The creation of the world is completed within one week.[11]
8. Humanity is destined to multiply, not to be decimated.[12]

---

8. Arguments 1–5 assembled by Hasel, "Significance of the Cosmology," 1–20; Hasel, "Polemic Nature," 81–102; Kapelrud, "Mythological Features," 178–96.

9. Concerning this thesis, Gunkel, *Creation and Chaos*, 78–80, translation of *Schöpfung und Chaos*, 115. Critical: Bauks, *Die Welt am Anfang*, 122–26, following Tsumura, *Earth and Waters*, 45–61.

10. Schmidt, *Alttestamentlicher Glaube*, 237. This argument is not yet found in the English translation *Faith of Old Testament*, 173–74 (translation of the fourth edition).

11. Hilbrands, " Länge der Schöpfungstage," 9–10.

12. Römer, "La création des hommes," 147–56.

REJECTION OF A POLEMICAL INTERPRETATION

Jan Christian Gertz represents an opposing view when he asserts that polemical language is entirely foreign to the creation account.[13] By that he not only refers to the *style*, but also to the *content* of the biblical statements. Whereas Horst-Dietrich Preuß could formulate that the stars were a mere afterthought, ranking even after the vegetables, Gertz interprets their position as outstanding since the fourth day is the center of the week. The presentation of their creation is the most detailed and complex section in the account, containing no sign of marginalization.[14] The avoidance of the designations "sun" and "moon" should not be traced back to a polemical intention, but is to be explained by the ambition of the author to systematize and categorize creation by means of generic terms and generic names. According to Gertz, this text is *Wissenschaftsprosa* ("scientific prose") with the aim of being "equally 'exact' relating to mythology as well as natural history."[15]

APOLOGETIC INTENTION WITHOUT POLEMICS?

Andreas Schüle shares his assessment concerning the nonpolemical style and content of Genesis 1. It appears "that the Israelite adoption of ancient mythology took place with little ideological-dogmatic intentions."[16] On the basis of his literary critical presuppositions, which cannot be debated here, Schüle treats the creation account as one of the "priestly" (P) texts, and contrasts it with Ezechiel and the latter chapters of Isaiah:

13. Gertz, "Antibabylonische Polemik," 145, 147: "gänzlich unpolemisch" (entirely unpolemical).

14. Gertz, "Antibabylonische Polemik," 145, referring to Preuß, *Verspottung*, 183: "Sie werden bei und von ihm nur unter 'ferner liefen' eingeordnet, rangieren sogar nach dem Gemüse."

15. "gleichermaßen mythologisch wie naturkundlich 'exakt'"; Gertz, *Antibabylonische Polemik*, 153, my translation; Rudimentary already in von Rad, *Genesis*, 75, referring to Genesis 2–3.

16. "dass die israelitische Aneignung antiker Mythologie kaum mit ideologisch-dogmatischen Absichten erfolgte," Schüle, *Urgeschichte*, 34.

> On the one hand the p-texts do not include polemics; on the contrary the plain, virtually unspectacular manner stands out, in which the priestly primeval history takes course. Any triumphant undertone is missing, which becomes immediately obvious, if compared to explicitly polemic texts like in Deuteroisaiah and Ezechiel.[17]

Having said that, Schüle understands the way of Israelite adoption of ancient mythology primarily on the background of "the apologetic interests of a natural theology":[18] By connecting the tradition of Israel to the textual world of its cultural environment, the account raises the claim of Israelite religion for acknowledgement in the multiethnic world of its time.

However, it has to be questioned if the orientation towards a coexistence of religions, as suggested by Schüle, can really be brought in line with the universalistic content of the passage itself. With Gertz one could talk about a *Weltentwurf* ("world concept"), differing radically from other concepts of that kind. Even though Gertz denies a polemic *intention* of the passage, at the end of his investigation he cannot exclude its apologetic *impact*: The text has contributed "to the disenchantment of nature."[19] Even Hermann Gunkel, for whom a direct dispute between a biblical "writer" and polytheistic texts was unthinkable, could hold on to an apologetic impact of the texts: "The Babylonian comprehension of things is understood to be mistaken."[20]

---

17. "Zum einen enthalten die P-Texte keinerlei Polemik; im Gegenteil fällt die schlichte, geradezu unspektakuläre Art auf, in der die priesterliche Urgeschichte abläuft. Jeder triumphalistische Unterton fehlt, was im Vergleich mit explizit polemischen Texten wie bei Deuterojesaja und Ezechiel unmittelbar deutlich wird," Schüle, *Prolog*, 63, 138, my translation.

18. "der apologetischen Interessen einer natürlichen Theologie," Schüle, *Prolog*, 64, for the following: 61, 64–65.

19. "Entzauberung der Natur": Gertz, "Antibabylonische Polemik," 155. Schmid, " Gegenwelt," 70–73, 80–85.

20. Gunkel, *Creation and Chaos*, 111. "Das babylonische Wissen ist als Irrtum erwiesen," Gunkel, *Schöpfung und Chaos*, 170. Gertz, "Antibabylonische Polemik," 139.

STYLE, CONTENT OR INTENDED IMPACT?

At this point, it becomes clear how important it is to keep our focus on the question of what we mean, when we use the term "polemics." Only this can lead to a sophisticated understanding of the present passage:

- Are we talking about polemical language or *style*?
- Are we talking about *content*, consciously formulated in reminiscence of foreign ideas—and by that not borrowing from them, but rejecting them?
- Are we talking about the critical *impact* or effect of a certain text—either intended or not?

There are indeed legitimate challenges to a supposed offensive-polemical intention behind Genesis 1:1–2:3. However, this alone does not question the apologetic intention behind the passage: the Israelite worldview is set in relation to foreign contemporary worldviews in a conspicuous way. Where deviations are visible, maybe even put into words, these foreign worldviews are scrutinized. In this way, foreign ideas are challenged to compete with the presupposed truth of the biblical version.

4

Narrative Apologetics
Apologetic Reflection on History

IN THE NARRATIVE TEXTS of the first canon part (Torah and Former Prophets), the claim to power of the God of creation soon comes into conflict with human-cultural hubris, as well as the authority of the gods of Egypt and Canaan. The demise of the kingdom of Israel and the Exile forces the historians to deal with a precursor of the question of theodicy: either God was not able to save, or he was unwilling... The claims to power of Babylonian and Assyrian deities are dealt with in the second canon part (Latter Prophets).

DISPUTE WITH HUMAN HUBRIS (PRIMEVAL HISTORY)

Some scholars have suggested an apologetic intention behind not only the creation account but also the whole of primeval history (Genesis 1–11), or at least parts of it. On the basis of his literary critical presuppositions, David Carr interprets the textual complex he assigns to "non-P" as the "counterwriting of its Mesopotamian counterpart": outline and motif of the Atraḫasis epic and other creation—flood narratives are taken over and intentionally refilled with decisively new content. A competing understanding of human existence and its relation to the divine world is thereby developed.[1] Despite serious objections, the tower of Babel narrative is widely understood as a "mock building account." According to this view, the story follows the outline of Mesopotamian building accounts, reshaping their themes and motifs in a polemical manner. The result is a

> highly stylized polemic against the name-making ideology and imperialistic endeavors of Mesopotamian kings.... Genesis 11:1–9 was originally composed as a diatribe against Mesopotamian royal ideology.[2]

Even though such "motif-historical" considerations seem to be disputable today,[3] the placement of the narrative within the context of the final form of Genesis reveals an apologetic bias that cannot be denied. In Gen 11:4 the builders reveal the plan of their hubris to "make a name for ourselves." In the subsequent chapter, YHWH promises Abram to "make your name great" (12:2). What the proud builders were not able to achieve out of their own strength, YHWH grants to his chosen servant as a free gift of blessing as the consequence of his humble obedience.[4]

THE GODS OF EGYPT

The narrative of the exodus from Egypt bears a clearly apologetic facet, since it is explained as a penal conviction of the gods of Egypt:

> For I will pass through the land of Egypt that night, and
> I will strike down every firstborn in the land of Egypt,

---

1. Carr, *Reading Fractures*, 245; Otto, "Brückenschläge," 91–92, n. 21, referring to the total primeval history and parts of the book of Exodus. Critical: Gertz, "Antibabylonische Polemik," 143, n. 20.

2. Giorgetti, "'Mock Building Account,'" 20, following Uehlinger, *Weltreich*.

3. See criticism in Schüle, *Prolog*, 401–16; Gertz, "Babel im Rücken," 29; also, more reluctantly, Seebass, *Genesis I*, 278.

4. Westermann, *Genesis*, 730; Dumbrell, *Covenant and Creation*, 59–61.

> both human beings and animals; on all the gods of Egypt
> I will execute judgments: I am the LORD (Exod 12:12).

YHWH cannot be compared with these other gods (15:11). Both Moses and his father-in-law Jethro later confess the superiority of YHWH over the other gods (Num 33:4, Exod 18:11).

The first and the ninth plagues are attacks on the most prominent fundaments of Egyptian life, the Nile and the sun. These could be understood as attacks on the Nile-god Hapi and Osiris, likewise connected to the Nile, as well as the sun-god Ra/Re, later Amon-Ra/Re. The frog plague could be an attack on the frog-goddess Ḥeqet/Ḥeqtit. Finally, it should not be forgotten that the Pharaoh and his eldest son (main targets of the judgment) were themselves worshipped as gods.[5]

The biblical texts emphasize the ineffectiveness of the Egyptian priests as representatives of their gods,[6] a tendency that can already be observed in Genesis 41:

> In the morning his spirit was troubled; so he sent and
> called for all the magicians of Egypt and all its wise men.
> Pharaoh told them his dreams, but there was no one who
> could interpret them to Pharaoh (Gen 41:8, v. 24).

Similar phenomena can be located in other parts of the Hebrew Bible.[7] Even though the worship of Baal has tremendous effects on the history of the northern kingdom of Israel, the priests as representatives of Baal are mocked by Elijah and humiliated in their powerlessness:

> Then they cried aloud and, as was their custom, they
> cut themselves with swords and lances until the blood
> gushed out over them. As midday passed, they raved on

---

5. Sarna, *Exploring Exodus*, 78–80; critical: Propp, *Exodus 1–18*, 400.

6. Exod 7:11–12, 22, 8:3, 14; 9:11. Ruppert, *Josephserzählung*, 76, talks about a polemical "humiliation of the Egyptian 'sages'" (*Beschämung der ägyptischen "Weisen"*). Ruppert observes how in Genesis 41 immanent, gentile wisdom is juxtaposed to the wisdom of Joseph, who receives all of his knowledge by YHWH.

7. Chazan, "Apologetics II," 416. See Preuß, *Verspottung*, 53–55.

until the time of the offering of the oblation, but there was no voice, no answer, and no response (1 Kgs 18:26–29).

And similar to Joseph, Daniel has to explain to king Nebuchadnezzar:

> No wise men, enchanters, magicians, or diviners can show to the king the mystery that the king is asking, but there is a God in heaven who reveals mysteries (Dan 2:27–28, vv. 2–12).

The purpose of the Exodus narrative is displayed in the total of twenty recognition formulas in the book complex of Exodus—Leviticus—Numbers.[8] There are ten formulas referring to Israel as recipient, and ten formulas referring to gentiles (Pharaoh, Egyptians, Jethro), the latter concentrated in the section about the deliverance out of Egypt and journey to Mount Sinai (Exod 6:27–18:27).[9]

No.	Book of Exodus	Recipient	Content
1.	6:7	Israel	I am the LORD your God, who has freed you from the burdens of the Egyptians
1.	7:5	**Egypt**	I am the LORD
2.	7:17	**Pharaoh**	I am the LORD
3.	8:10	**Pharaoh**	there is no one like the LORD our God
4.	8:22	**Pharaoh**	I the LORD am in this land.
5.	9:14	**Pharaoh**	there is no one like me in all the earth[113]
6.	9:29	**Pharaoh**	the earth is the LORD's
2.	10:2	Israel	I am the LORD

---

8. For the unity of the book (complex) of Exodus—Leviticus—Numbers, see Koorevaar, "Torah as One," 1–19; Koorevaar, "Exodus—Levitikus—Numeri," 87–131; Koorevaar, "Books of Exodus," 423–53, based on Wenham, *Numbers*, 15–18.

9. The recognition formulas referring to gentiles as recipients are marked with bold font in the chart.

10. The translation of Exod 9:14, 29 prefers the word "earth" to "land," in contrast to Exod 8:22, where the land of Goshen is in view. However, it cannot be said for sure, which meaning is correct. Houtman, *Exodus*, 10.

7.	11:7	**Pharaoh**	the LORD makes a distinction between Egypt and Israel
8.	14:4	**Egypt**	I am the LORD
9.	14:8	**Egypt**	I am the LORD
3.	16:6	Israel	it was the LORD who brought you out of the land of Egypt
4.	16:12	Israel	I am the LORD your God
10.	18:11	**Jethro**	the LORD is greater than all gods
5.	29:46	Israel	I am the LORD their God, who brought them out of the land of Egypt that I might dwell among them; I am the LORD their God
6.	31:13	Israel	I, the LORD, sanctify you

Leviticus

7.	23:43	Israel	I made the people of Israel live in booths when I brought them out of the land of Egypt: I am the LORD your God

Numbers

8.	14:34	Israel	my displeasure
9.	16:28	Israel	the LORD has sent me to do all these works; it has not been of my own accord
10.	16:30	Israel	these men have despised the LORD

Within this book complex,[11] the number ten has a significant importance as the number of completeness. The commandments

---

11. It could be objected that the number of ten expressions within such a large textual scope can hardly be the result of purposeful planning. However, it can be substantiated that counting schemes like these are not unlikely. In Num 14:22, it is said that the Israelites "have tested me these ten times and have not obeyed my voice." According to rabbinic interpretation (*b. Ar.* 15a–b) this has to be referred to: "two at the sea" (Exod 14:11, 30), "two because of water" (Exod 15:24, 17:3), "two because of manna" (Exod 16:20, 27), "two because of the quails" (Exod 16:3; Num 11:4), "one in connection with the golden calf" (Exod 32), and "one in the wilderness of Paran" (Num 14:3). Since Exod 14:30 reveals no direct connection, it makes sense to replace it by Num 11:1, Dillmann, *Numeri*, 77; see Seebass, *Numeri* 2, 120 for an alternative, non-verbal interpretation.

of Sinai are *'ăseret haddəḇārîm* "ten words" (Exod 34:28) and the number of plagues is ten. "YHWH has gone to his utmost in his case against Pharaoh and Pharaoh has resisted to the utmost before succumbing."[12] Building on that, it can be deduced that YHWH not only goes to the utmost in order to free his people, but also in order to mediate knowledge to the Egyptians.[13] YHWH intervenes in world history in order to impart knowledge about his universal power both with the Israelites and with the non-Israelites.

The only retrospective recognition formula can be found in Exodus 18:11, where the Midianite priest Jethro is quoted by the words:

> Now I know that the LORD is greater than all gods, because he delivered the people from the Egyptians, when they dealt arrogantly with them.

For Christian Frevel, the peculiar importance of these words lies in the fact "that this is the *only* prolonged confession of a non-Israelite to YHWH in the Pentateuch."[14] This outstanding confession seems to be an adequate literary solution for the tension between the hopeful recognition formulas and the persistent stubbornness of Pharaoh's heart. Jethro, the Midianite, functions as a substitute for the Egyptian king.[15] With Jethro, the ethnic boundary (limiting the recognition formula to Egypt) is transgressed, because Pharaoh's reaction to the miracles of YHWH remains far from adequate.

The consequence of Jethro's confession is the termination of any further worship of other gods except for YHWH—be it the gods of the ancestors, the gods of the Egyptians, or the gods of Canaan (gods of the Amorites). Besides clear exclusive formulations in the "ten words" (Exod 20:3, Deut 5:7), the covenant renewal at

---

12. Houtman, *Exodus*, 68.
13. Riecker, *Priestervolk*, 135–139.
14. "dass es das *einzige* ausgedehntere Bekenntnis eines Nicht-Israeliten zu Jahwe im Pentateuch ist," Christian Frevel, "'Jetzt habe ich erkannt'," 20.
15. Enger, *Adoptivkinder Abrahams*, 349; Propp, *Exodus 1–18*, 630.

Shechem exemplifies the practical realization of this inescapable alternative:

> "Now if you are unwilling to serve the LORD, choose this day whom you will serve, whether the gods your ancestors served in the region beyond the River or the gods of the Amorites in whose land you are living; but as for me and my household, we will serve the LORD." Then the people answered, "Far be it from us that we should forsake the LORD to serve other gods; for it is the LORD our God who brought us and our ancestors up from the land of Egypt, out of the house of slavery, and who did those great signs in our sight" (Josh 24:14–17, v. 2).

THE GODS OF CANAAN

The canonical historiography of Israel contains early polemics not only against the religious-cultural system of Egypt, but also against the culture of Canaan:

> You shall not do as they do in the land of Egypt, where you lived, and you shall not do as they do in the land of Canaan, to which I am bringing you. You shall not follow their statutes (Lev 18:3).

This also concerns Canaanite religious practices:

> take care that you are not snared into imitating them, after they have been destroyed before you: do not inquire concerning their gods, saying, "How did these nations worship their gods? I also want to do the same." (Deut 12:30).

Even though the Philistines do not belong to the seven nations of Canaan, they live within the boundaries of the promised land and pose a threat to the young nation of Israel from the outset. The conflict between Yahweh the God of Israel and Dagon the god of the Philistines is described at great length in 1 Samuel 5. Dagon succumbs, and as in Leviticus 18, the memory of the sojourn in

Egypt plays an important role here. When the Philistines learn that the ark of Yahweh has come to the camp they react with fear:

> Woe to us! Who can deliver us from the power of these mighty gods? These are the gods who struck the Egyptians with every sort of plague in the wilderness (1 Sam 4:8).

After the presence of the ark causes a great plague among the Philistines, their diviners give the advice to honor YHWH, again drawing a parallel to the events in Egypt:[16]

> give glory to the God of Israel; perhaps he will lighten his hand on you and your gods and your land. Why should you harden your hearts as the Egyptians and Pharaoh hardened their hearts? After he had made fools of them, did they not let the people go, and they departed? (1 Sam 6:5–6).

Only in the course of later history, in the times of Elijah, do we come across a direct confrontation between Baal and YHWH. However, there might be a longer prehistory of hidden polemics in the Exodus narrative and the books of Joshua and Judges. Whenever YHWH is described as warrior and king, lord of the storm, lord of the sea and lord of death, we could understand these descriptions as an intentional adoption of the attributes of Baal, in order to challenge his claim to power from the outset, "as part of a polemical strategy whereby Yahweh established His exclusive right to His people's worship and loyalty."[17]

---

16. Preuß, *Verspottung*, 74–80.
17. Chisholm, "Polemic against Baalism," 283, referring to Exod 9:22–25, 15:8, 10, 12, 19:16–19; Deut 33:26; Josh 10:11; Judg 5:4–5; 1 Sam 2:2, 10, 7:10, 12:16–18; Pss 18:5–20, 32, 29:3–10 et al.

YHWH AND THE DEMISE OF HIS PEOPLE— THEOLOGICAL MODELS FOR THE INTERPRETATION OF HISTORY

Israelite historiography has to face the problem that neither the people nor its kings can serve as the ideal of an obedient life, dedicated solely to their God, as demanded in their holy scriptures (Deut 4:6–8, 17:17; Judg 2:11–23).[18] However, these seemingly disparaging parts of history are not blotted out of history. On the contrary, the unfaithfulness of the individual rulers of Israel is emphasized in their religious evaluation. With the description of the downfall of the northern (2 Kgs 17:7–23) and southern kingdoms of Israel (23:26–27, 24:2–4) comes an extensive retribution between God and his people. The catastrophe is interpreted as the judgment of the unfaithfulness of Israel and Judah, which is implemented through the use of foreign nations to execute the verdict against his own people:

> The LORD sent against him bands of the Chaldeans, bands of the Arameans, bands of the Moabites, and bands of the Ammonites; he sent them against Judah to destroy it, according to the word of the LORD that he spoke by his servants the prophets. Surely this came upon Judah at the command of the LORD, to remove them out of his sight, for the sins of Manasseh, for all that he had committed and also for the innocent blood that he had shed; for he filled Jerusalem with innocent blood, and the LORD was not willing to pardon (2 Kgs 24:2–4).

In the chapter "The Nations as Yahweh's Partners" in *Theology of the Old Testament,* Walter Brueggemann observes a delicate balance in the relationship between YHWH and the four superpowers of Old Testament times (Egypt, Assyria, Babylon, and Persia). Each nation has a limited mandate, but often gives in to the temptation to abuse its power.[19] The image of YHWH as king of this earth

---

18. See Chazan, "Apologetics II," 416.
19. Brueggemann, *Theology,* 492–527.

transcends the simple idea of a power struggle between national deities.

The suspicion that the demise of his own people can be interpreted as the failure of the national deity YHWH—and his apparent inferiority to the gods of the enemies—is a broadly based biblical motif:

> I feared provocation by the enemy, for their adversaries might misunderstand and say, "Our hand is triumphant; it was not the LORD who did all this." (Deut 32:27).

The provision in the wilderness, in particular, reflects the capability of YHWH as the national deity of Israel. Even though he has the right to devastate his unfaithful people after the golden calf incident, he backs off from this final step, which would endanger his reputation among the nations.

> otherwise the land from which you have brought us might say, "Because the LORD was not able to bring them into the land that he promised them, and because he hated them, he has brought them out to let them die in the wilderness" (Deut 9:28).[20]

Such explanations of history, deviating from the salvation history of YHWH, are not only feared hypothetically. There are alternative historical models circulating among the people, as can be seen with the "salvation history of the queen of heaven"[21] of the Judeans, which have fled to Egypt:

> Instead, we will do everything that we have vowed, make offerings to the queen of heaven and pour out libations to her, just as we and our ancestors, our kings and our officials, used to do in the towns of Judah and in the streets of Jerusalem. We used to have plenty of food, and prospered, and saw no misfortune. But from the time we stopped making offerings to the queen of heaven

---

20. See Deut 1:27; Exod 14:11–12, 16:3, 17:3, 32:12; Num 14:16; Josh 7:9; and Ps 78:19.

21. Holladay, *Jeremiah 2*, 286, interprets the queen of heaven as Astarte and talks about the "counter-argument of the *Heilsgeschichte* of Astarte."

> and pouring out libations to her, we have lacked everything and have perished by the sword and by famine (Jer 44:17–18).

According to this understanding, history has proven that precisely the allegiance to YHWH is the very cause that leads to destruction, especially when it endangers peace with the most powerful gods of this world.

Apologetics against such interpretation models has a clear outward direction against distinctive gentile religiosity, even if it is practiced by those within the boundaries of Israel's own land.

THE IMPACT OF MODELS FOR THE INTERPRETATION OF HISTORY

In his classic volume *After Virtue,* Alisdair MacIntyre considers the question "Of what story or stories do I find myself a part?" as one of the key elements of human existence.[22] This evaluation points to the enormous impact of historical interpretation models on the religion and ethics of Old Testament readers of all times. Historical-theological based apologetics is by far more than a discussion among historians about the past, or as Bob Becking puts it, regarding the competing historical interpretation models presented in Jeremiah 44:

> The issue behind the discussion is not an attempt to reach an agreement on the most probable reconstruction of past events. . . . The core element in the polemic is the question: . . . What moral and religious standards are to be upheld?[23]

Theological interpretation of history transforms the identity and behavior of the individual reader as well as the believing community. Its persuasive power can hardly be overestimated.

---

22. MacIntyre, *After Virtue,* 216. Provan, *Seriously Dangerous Religion,* 1–20.

23. Becking, "Jeremiah 44," 261.

5

Prophetic Apologetics
YHWH as Apologist

NARRATIVE APOLOGETICS IS EXCEEDINGLY effective and memorable, if it refers to the witnesses of nature and history. However, in most cases, it remains an indirect approach. A direct attack of YHWH against foreign gods on the other hand is executed via his mouthpieces, the prophets, albeit distinctively prepared in the book of Deuteronomy.

PREPARATION IN THE BOOK OF DEUTERONOMY

Serving idols is portrayed in Deuteronomy as judgment and punishment:

> There you will serve other gods made by human hands, objects of wood and stone that neither see, nor hear, nor eat, nor smell (Deut 4:28; 2 Kgs 19:18; Judg 6:31).

Human-made idols are helpless objects without any sensory perception. When the song of Moses degrades the gods of the nations as *loʾ-ʾēl*, "not-god," and *hebel*, "vapor" (32:21), it does not deny their existence. When v. 17 describes *šēdîm*, "demons," and *ʾĕlōhîm*, "gods, divine ones," there is an invisible reality, more than dead wood or metal. It is not their existence that is challenged, but their effectiveness. The Old Testament "regarded the gods not as nothing, but as good for nothing."[1]

A secondary attack is aimed at the worship of gods in the form of "the sun or the moon or any of the host of heaven" (Deut 17:3). Even the astral deities are powerless. If they have any connection to the nations of the world, it is entirely dependent on the permission of YHWH:

> And when you look up to the heavens and see the sun, the moon, and the stars, all the host of heaven, do not be led astray and bow down to them and serve them, things that the LORD your God has allotted to all the peoples everywhere under heaven (Deut 4:19).

Like trust in material goods, the worship of those deities amounts to a renouncement of the true God and creator. On this basis, Job can confess in the third canon part:

> If I have made gold my trust, or called fine gold my confidence; if I have rejoiced because my wealth was great, or because my hand had gotten much; if I have looked at the sun when it shone, or the moon moving in splendor, and my heart has been secretly enticed, and my mouth has kissed my hand; this also would be an iniquity to be punished by the judges, for I should have been false to God above (Job 31:24–28; Jer 8:2; Zeph 1:5)

Opposed to that, YHWH presents himself as the epitome of effective power:

---

1. Schmidt, *Faith*, 279, translation of "galten die Götter nicht als 'nichts,' sondern als 'nichtsnutzig,'" Schmidt, *Glaube*, 433, referring to Isa 41:24, 44:10 et al. Like many before him Smith, "Polemic of Biblical Monotheism," 203–5, distinguishes between claims of exclusivity of YHWH "alone" and no god "apart from, besides" (Deut 4:35; 2 Kgs 19:15, 19; Isa 37:16, 20; Neh 9:6; Ps 86:10; 2 Sam 7:22; 1 Chr 17:20) and claims that all other deities are "not," "nothings," or "dead" (Deut 4:39; 1 Sam 2:2; Jer 16:19–20; Ps 96:5; 1 Chr 16:26; Ps 82:7). See pp. 203, n. 2 for further literature.

> See now that I, even I, am he; there is no god besides me.
> I kill and I make alive; I wound and I heal; and no one
> can deliver from my hand (Deut 32:39).

The sovereign kingship of YHWH is also displayed in Isaiah 24–27. Referring to parallels in KTU 1.1–1.6, William Barker finds evidence that these chapters might have been designed as an intended attack on the power of Baal, Mot, and their adherents.[2]

APOLOGETICS IN THE PROPHETIC BOOKS BETWEEN DEUTERONOMY AND WISDOM LITERATURE

The prophetic books of the Hebrew Bible develop their polemics against foreign gods much more extensively than the book of Deuteronomy.[3] Polemic statements in the prophetic books can be subsumed under the themes of creation, figural representation, prophecy, and moral offenses, as well as judgment.

Gerhard von Rad identifies a connection between prophetic polemics against foreign gods and the mindset of wisdom literature, dedicating an entire chapter to the theme of "The Polemic against Idols" in his volume *Wisdom in Israel*.[4]

This connection can be illustrated by Psalm 135 (linked to Psalm 115) and its recourse to Jeremiah 10. Here it is not only the linkage between a prophetic book and the third canon part, but the content of Jeremiah 10 also brings together prophetic polemics and the question of wisdom:[5]

> There is none like you, O LORD; you are great, and
> your name is great in might. Who would not fear you,

---

2. Barker, *Isaiah's Kingship Polemic*.

3. Main references are Isa 40:12–31, 41:6–7, 21–29, 42:8–9, 17, 44:9–20, 45:14–17, 20–21, 46:1–7, 48:3–5; Jer 10:1–16; Hab 2:18–19.

4. Ammann, *Götter für die Toren*, 1; referring to von Rad, *Weisheit in Israel*, 229–39, first edition translated as *Wisdom in Israel*, 177–85.

5. See Ammann, *Götter für die Toren*, 137, for the direction of textual dependences. Look to the chapter on wisdom below for a definition of "wisdom," and the idea of including the book of Psalms in this category.

O King of the nations? For that is your due; among all the wise ones of the nations and in all their kingdoms there is no one like you. They are both stupid and foolish; the instruction given by idols is no better than wood! (Jer 10:6–8).

THE SPECIAL STATUS OF THE CREATOR

In their apologetic dispute, the biblical prophets start with creation. Idols are material artifacts, created by craftspeople. YHWH, however, is the creator of heaven and earth.[6] Therefore, there is a fundamental difference between the God of creation and all other beings:

> Beaten silver is brought from Tarshish, and gold from Uphaz. They are the work of the artisan and of the hands of the goldsmith; their clothing is blue and purple; they are all the product of skilled workers. But the LORD is the true God; he is the living God and the everlasting King. At his wrath the earth quakes, and the nations cannot endure his indignation. Thus shall you say to them: The gods who did not make the heavens and the earth shall perish from the earth and from under the heavens. It is he who made the earth by his power, who established the world by his wisdom, and by his understanding stretched out the heavens (Jer 10:9–12; Ps 96:5).

The statement in verse 11 that all gods "who did not make the heaven and the earth shall perish from the earth" is formulated in Aramaic. Jeremiah may have intentionally employed the more international language because it was used for diplomatic communication and trade. Then verse 11 would not be a gloss, as commonly assumed, but intentionally placed by Jeremiah in the center of this section (Jer 10:1–16). The readers are prepared and encouraged to proclaim such a message to the Babylonian emperors as a "polemical summary" of Israelite theology.[7]

6. Ramm, "Apologetic," 17; Bruce, *Apostolic Defence*, 27–28.
7. Reid, "'Thus You Will Say,'" 221–38.

THE FIGURAL DEPICTION OF GODS

The pictographic representation of gods by idols is open to attack in several ways. In his investigation on the reception of Old Testament polemics in Jewish literature in the Greco-Roman culture, Nijay Gupta lists five points of attack, which he finds in Psalm 135:15-17 (categories 1, 2, 3, 5) and the apocryphal Epistle of Jeremiah 26-27 (category 4):

> (1) the idol is a human creation; (2) the idol is not alive; (3) the idol does not have natural senses (seeing, hearing, speaking); (4) the idol cannot move; and (5) the idol is inefficacious (i.e., useless).[8]

As will be shown below, it is possible to also identify category 4 ("the idol cannot move") within the prophet canon. However, category 3 ("the idol does not have natural senses") seems to appear only in the wisdom canon.

(1) The Idol is a Human Creation

The most ironic and picturesque description of the crafting of idols can be found in Isaiah 44:9-20, which emphasizes the very destructibility of its own material.

> Half of it he burns in the fire; over this half he roasts meat, eats it and is satisfied. He also warms himself and says, "Ah, I am warm, I can feel the fire!" The rest of it he makes into a god, his idol, bows down to it and worships it; he prays to it and says, "Save me, for you are my god!" (Isa 44:16-17).

---

8. Gupta, "'They Are Not Gods!,'" 711; Smith, "Polemic of Biblical Monotheism," 231, mentioning the polemic categories of "parody, poetry and the past." On p. 233 he refers to Isa 44 and Clifford, "Function of Idol Passage," 463, and Holter, *Second Isaiah's Idol*, 127-212. See Dick, "Prophetic Parodies," 1-53, in dependence on Dohmen, *Bilderverbot*, especially 36-37; Petry, *Entgrenzung JHWHs*, 97-384; Roth, "For Life," 21-47; Berlejung, *Theologie der Bilder*, 315-413.

(2) The Idol is not Alive

The lifelessness of the idols is accentuated in the observation that there is no *rûaḥ* "spirit" in them (Jer 10:14, Hab 2:19; Ps 135:17). Jeremiah compares their dumbness to other man-made objects:

> Their idols are like scarecrows in a cucumber field, and they cannot speak; they have to be carried, for they cannot walk. Do not be afraid of them, for they cannot do evil, nor is it in them to do good (Jer 10:5).

Habakkuk warns his audience not to try to make them speak. It will not lead to success, but instead evoke the wrath of God (2:4, 3:2, 5–9).

> Alas for you who say to the wood, "Wake up!" to silent stone, "Rouse yourself!" Can it teach? See, it is gold and silver plated, and there is no breath in it at all (Hab 2:19).

(3) The Idol Does not Have Natural Senses

Indirectly, Hab 2:19 might refer to the sense of hearing. The absence of the idols' natural senses is only explicitly expressed in the third canon part. Psalm 115:5–7 contains an almost complete list of the senses: they cannot see, hear, smell, or feel.

> Why should the nations say, "Where is their God?"
> ³ Our God is in the heavens; he does whatever he pleases.
> ⁴ Their idols are silver and gold, the work of human hands.
> ⁵ They have mouths, but do not speak; eyes, but do not see.
> ⁶ They have ears, but do not hear;
> noses, but do not smell.
> ⁷ They have hands, but do not feel;
> feet, but do not walk;
> they make no sound in their throats.
> ⁸ Those who make them are like them;
> so are all who trust in them (Ps 115:2–8).

This list occurs in a shorter form in Psalm 135:15–18. In the chiastic structure of this psalm, the idol polemics is opposed to the description of the incomparable creative powers of YHWH (135:5–7).[9] This passage begins by taking up the confession of Jethro from Exodus 18:11 (Ps 135:5, see the "signs and wonders" of the Exodus in vv. 7–8; Jer 10:6):

> For I know that the LORD is great; our Lord is above all gods. Whatever the LORD pleases he does, in heaven and on earth, in the seas and all deeps. He it is who makes the clouds rise at the end of the earth; he makes lightnings for the rain and brings out the wind from his storehouses (Ps 135:5–7).

The description of YHWH's authority over weather in v. 7 (Jer 10:13) is especially linked to the description of idols via wordplay (*'śh*, "to do, make," in Pss 135:15, 18 and *rûaḥ* "spirit, wind" in v. 17). YHWH is not made, but a maker. Not only does he have a *rûaḥ*, he is the commander of the *rûaḥ* on this earth.

(4) The Idol cannot Move

The four senses in Psalm 115 (seeing, hearing, smelling, feeling) are framed with remarks on the dumbness (speaking) and immobility (walking) of the idols. The consequence of the latter is that the nations have to "carry about their wooden idols" (Isa 45:20). If they need to go on a journey, the idols are loaded onto the shoulders of humans or animals.

> Bel bows down, Nebo stoops, their idols are on beasts and cattle; these things you carry are loaded as burdens on weary animals. They stoop, they bow down together; they cannot save the burden, but themselves go into captivity.... They lift it to their shoulders, they carry it, they set it in its place, and it stands there; it cannot move from its place. If one cries out to it, it does not answer or save anyone from trouble (Isa 46:1–2, 7).

---

9. Weber, *Werkbuch Psalmen II*, 326–27; Emanuel, *From Bards to Biblical*, 191–93.

Even the idols of Bel and Nebo, the traditional Babylonian gods, must be carried by animals. The idea of the idols becoming a burden is also true in a figurative sense. Just as the animals get exhausted from the weight on their backs, so too are humans wearied by the work of crafting their gods. The idols bring weakness into the life of their creators:

> The ironsmith fashions it and works it over the coals, shaping it with hammers, and forging it with his strong arm; he becomes hungry and his strength fails, he drinks no water and is faint (Isa 44:12).

Still on a figurative level, YHWH contrasts his active "carrying" to the passivity of the idols "being carried":

> Listen to me, O house of Jacob, all the remnant of the house of Israel, who have been borne by me from your birth, carried from the womb; even to your old age I am he, even when you turn gray I will carry you. I have made, and I will bear; I will carry and will save (Isa 36:3-4).

Isaiah can take up this image of provision and care from Deuteronomy 1:31, where YHWH is said to have carried his people all the way through the wilderness "just as one carries a child."

Another consequence of the immobility of the idols is revealed in their inability to balance their own weight. It means disgrace for an idol to tip over, and there is always the danger of losing one's head or other extremities during the fall (1 Sam 5:3–5). A skilled artisan is needed to set up an image "that will not topple" (Isa 40:20). Eventually, it is necessary to "fasten it with hammer and nails so that it cannot move" (Jer 10:4; Isa 41:7).

(5) The Idol is Inefficacious

The description so far culminates in the resulting realization that these idols are nothing and can do nothing. For Jeremiah they are *hebel* "vapor" (Jer 10:15; Deut 31:21). Similar to Elijah (1 Kgs 18:27), Isaiah mocks their ineffectiveness by trying to provoke their anger:

do good, or do harm, that we may be afraid and terrified. You, indeed, are nothing and your work is nothing at all; whoever chooses you is an abomination (Isa 41:23b–24).

The only ones who can get angry however, are their adherents. Eventually even they will be exposed as stupid and put to shame (Jer 10:14). Whatever they expect from their efforts, they are doomed from the outset. They will be lead astray; their soul will not be saved (Isa 44:20). Like the objects of their worship they are nothing and they will get nothing out of it:

> All who make idols are nothing, and the things they delight in do not profit; their witnesses neither see nor know. And so they will be put to shame. Who would fashion a god or cast an image that can do no good? Look, all its devotees shall be put to shame; the artisans too are merely human. Let them all assemble, let them stand up; they shall be terrified, they shall all be put to shame (Isa 44:9–11).

PROPHECY (FUTURE EVENTS)

When gods come into conflict with one another, the superiority of a god's power is determined and demonstrated through the act of miracles. For example, supernatural *deeds* were prevalent in the exodus from Egypt and the power struggle on Mount Carmel. Within the writing prophets, supernatural *knowledge* (prophecy) plays a key role in such conflicts about the legitimization of:

a. the prophet as representative (true or false prophet)
b. the message of the prophet (divine word or human invention)
c. the god of the prophet (living or dead god)

From a Hebrew perspective, the fulfillment of prophecy alone is not the final legitimization of the representative. Even if "the omens or the portents declared by them take place," their message has to be in accordance with the Torah (Deut 13:2–4). However, if the predicted event does not occur, the message of the prophecy is proven wrong:

> If a prophet speaks in the name of the LORD but the thing does not take place or prove true, it is a word that the LORD has not spoken. The prophet has spoken it presumptuously; do not be frightened by it (Deut 18:22).

Obviously, in many cases, the representatives of other gods are not able to predict anything. Their errors and their general inability turn them into a laughing stock:

> Set forth your case, says the LORD; bring your proofs, says the King of Jacob. Let them bring them, and tell us what is to happen. Tell us the former things, what they are, so that we may consider them, and that we may know their outcome; or declare to us the things to come. Tell us what is to come hereafter, that we may know that you are gods (Isa 41:21–23a, 42:9, 45:21, 48:14).

In contrast, YHWH presents his ability, not only to predict future events, but also to bring them about: "My purpose shall stand, and I will fulfill my intention" (Isa 46:10, 43:12).

MORAL OFFENSES BY THE REPRESENTATIVES

A decision about the legitimacy of a god's representative (true or false prophet, prophet of a living or dead god) can be made not only on the level of truth (right and wrong), but also on a moral level (good and evil). Prophetic apologetics strive to expose not only the error of false prophets, but also their wickedness.[10] They are promised doom and disgrace, particularly when they take money for glossing over the sins of God's people:[11]

> Thus says the LORD concerning the prophets who lead my people astray, who cry "Peace" when they have something to eat, but declare war against those who put

---

10. Jer 8:10–11, 14:13–18, 23:9–40, chap. 28; Lam 2:14; Ezek 12:24, chap. 13; Zeph 3:4; Zech 13:2, 4; 1 Kgs 22:19–23.

11. Wolff, *Prophetische Alternativen*, 70–83; Kraus, *Prophetie*, 104–15.

nothing into their mouths. Therefore it shall be night to you, without vision, and darkness to you, without revelation. The sun shall go down upon the prophets, and the day shall be black over them; the seers shall be disgraced, and the diviners put to shame; they shall all cover their lips, for there is no answer from God. But as for me, I am filled with power, with the spirit of the LORD, and with justice and might, to declare to Jacob his transgression and to Israel his sin (Mic 3:5–8; Isa 30:10).

JUDGMENT ON FOREIGN GODS

The extermination of idols from Israel[12] and foreign gods from this earth is proclaimed as a settled matter:

> The LORD will be terrible against them; he will shrivel all the gods of the earth, and to him shall bow down, each in its place, all the coasts and islands of the nations (Zeph 2:11; Jer 10:11, 15).

The oracles against the nations by Jeremiah, in particular, are not only meant challenge the nations and their kings, but also explicitly their gods. In Egypt, YHWH will attack the king of gods, Amun/Amon of Thebes (biblical name of the city: *nō'*), and other gods.

> The LORD of hosts, the God of Israel, said: See, I am bringing punishment upon Amon of Thebes, and Pharaoh, and Egypt and her gods and her kings, upon Pharaoh and those who trust in him (Jer 46:25, 43:12; Isa 19:1; Ezek 30:13).

The Moabite god Chemosh shall wander off in disgrace:

> Chemosh shall go out into exile, with his priests and his attendants.... Then Moab shall be ashamed of Chemosh (Jer 48:7, 13).

The same fate awaits the Ammonite national god and all of his priests: "For Milcom shall go into exile, with his priests and his

---

12. Isa 2:18, 20; Jer 51:18; Ezek 6:6; Zech 13:2.

attendants" (Jer 49:3, v. 1).¹³ YHWH will furthermore afflict Marduk (probably biblical "Merodach"), head of the Babylonian pantheon, oftentimes called Bel ("lord, master") and his son Nabu (biblical "Nebo," Isa 46:1).¹⁴

> Declare among the nations and proclaim, set up a banner and proclaim, do not conceal it, say: Babylon is taken, Bel is put to shame, Merodach is dismayed. Her images are put to shame, her idols are dismayed (Jer 50:2, 51:44; Isa 21:9).

The theological climax of this judgement can be found outside of the writing prophets in Psalm 82. The New Testament scholar John Dominic Crossan once labeled this Psalm "the single most important text in the entire Christian Bible."¹⁵ The *ĕlōhîm* "gods," the *bǝnê 'elyôn*, "children of the most high,"¹⁶ were appointed by YHWH to govern the nations (Pss 29:1, 58:2, 89:6–7), but now they have failed:

> "How long will you judge unjustly and show partiality to the wicked? Give justice to the weak and the orphan; maintain the right of the lowly and the destitute. Rescue the weak and the needy; deliver them from the hand of the wicked." They have neither knowledge nor understanding, they walk around in darkness; all the foundations of the earth are shaken (Ps 82:2–5).

Now they have to die like humans. God judges them and enlarges his established dominion. He is no longer just confirmed as ruler of the territory of Israel, but the king of all the nations:

> I say, "You are gods, children of the Most High, all of you; nevertheless, you shall die like mortals, and fall like

---

13. In Jer 49:1, 3 *mlkm* usually is not taken as *malkām* "their king" (MT), but with LXX, Syr, Vg as *milkōm* "Milkom," see Scheurer, *Altes Testament*, 360, n. 32.

14. Scheurer, *Altes Testament*, 357–74.

15. Crossan, *Birth of Christianity*, 575; McCann, "Single Most Important Text," 63–75; Preuß, *Verspottung*, 105–17, 248–53, for other Psalms.

16. For the interpretation of "children of the most high," Koorevaar, "Psalm 82," 57–69; Trotter, "Death," 221–39 et al.

any prince." Rise up, O God, judge the earth; for all the nations belong to you! (Ps 82:6–8).

6

Wisdom Apologetics
Interpretation of Life and Praise of God

IN A BROADER SENSE, the heading "wisdom" includes all the books of the third part of the Hebrew canon (Ruth, Psalms, Job, Proverbs, Ecclesiastes, Song of Songs, Lamentations, Daniel, Esther, Ezra–Nehemiah and Chronicles) since they are marked by a "wisdom-scribe viewpoint."[1] The term "wisdom apologetics" was coined by Horst Dietrich Preuß, who uses it in a rather narrow sense to refer specifically to chapters 13–15 in the Book of Wisdom.[2] Here, it will be used in a broader canonical sense to refer to the third canon part of the Hebrew Bible.

As already indicated, the third canon part takes up the polemic in the prophets against foreign gods and processes it in a (1) doxological-confessional and (2) narrative way. Wisdom also means (3) reflecting upon one's own thinking during confrontation with the intention of self-reassurance. This leads to very fundamental questions of (4) value and purpose of belief in God.

---

1. Steinberg, *Ketuvim,* 469–84 talks about a "weisheitlich-schriftgelehrte Sichtweise" (p. 469, my translation); Gordis, "Religion," 365.

2. Preuß, *Verspottung,* 267.

PUBLIC DISPUTE (DOXOLOGICAL-CONFESSIONAL)

Like the prophets, the psalms celebrate the affirmed supremacy of the true God above the idols and foreign gods.

> For great is the LORD, and greatly to be praised; he is to be revered above all gods. For all the gods of the peoples are idols, but the LORD made the heavens (Pss 96:4-5, 86:8, 89:7 [6], 95:3, 97:7; 135:5).

In the theology of the Psalms, this affirmation does not happen behind closed doors, but in public, even in dispute with the nations. Here, Israel is called to openly proclaim YHWH and his supremacy over the gods among the nations. The nations, in turn, are called to praise him too:

> Declare his glory among the nations, his marvelous works among all the peoples.... Ascribe to the LORD, O families of the peoples, ascribe to the LORD glory and strength. Ascribe to the LORD the glory due his name; bring an offering, and come into his courts. Worship the LORD in holy splendor; tremble before him, all the earth. Say among the nations, "The LORD is king! The world is firmly established; it shall never be moved. He will judge the peoples with equity" (Pss 96:3, 7-10, 9:12 [11], 47:2, 66:8, 97:6-9, 105:1, 117:1).

Besides such invitations to others, the psalmist plans himself to openly reveal his loyalty to the word of YHWH before the rulers of this world. For such an undertaking he prays for God's grace:

> Then I shall have an answer for those who taunt me, for I trust in your word. Do not take the word of truth utterly out of my mouth, for my hope is in your ordinances.... I will also speak of your decrees before kings, and shall not be put to shame (Pss 119:42-43, 46, 18:50 [49], 57:10 [9], 108:4 [3]).

It is disputed in how far these testified intentions are actually put into practice. Robert Martin-Archard challenges the conclusion that this has to be understood as an attempt at proselytization:

> The major preoccupation of the psalmists was not with propaganda for Yahweh directed to the heathen. Their psalms were designed to be used by the Jerusalemite community and concern Israel and not the nations.[3]

However, the effect of these words on the relationship of the praying individual to his different-minded neighbors and his behavior towards them is not to be underestimated.

PUBLIC DISPUTE (NARRATIVE)

The book of Esther deals with the problem of hatred towards Jews, but restricts itself to the ethnic level. Horst Dietrich Preuß notices that there is no religious mockery in the book of Esther.[4]

On the other hand, Daniel and his friends put into practice what is liturgically called for in the book of Psalms. The book of Daniel advocates the sovereign dominion of the God of Israel over world history by means of narratives, testimonies and visions. The most powerful leaders at the time of the exile and their savants[5] are repeatedly humiliated by this God and have to confess his greatness as "God of gods and Lord of kings" (Dan 2:47).[6] The climax of the controversy is the challenge of Nebuchadnezzar at the fiery furnace: "Who is the god that will deliver you out of my hands?" The answer comes promptly:

> we have no need to present a defense to you in this matter. If our God whom we serve is able to deliver us from the furnace of blazing fire and out of your hand, O king, let him deliver us. But if not, be it known to you, O king,

---

3. Martin-Archard, *Light to Nations*, 58. For the current state of research, see Riecker, *Priestervolk*, 187–88.

4. Preuß, *Verspottung*, 255–54; see Levinson, "Apologetik I," 47–50.

5. Ramm, "Apologetic," 18. Lenzi, "Secrecy," 347–48.

6. Dan 3:28–29, 31–33 [4:1–3], 4:31–34 [34–37], 6:26–27 [27–28].

that we will not serve your gods and we will not worship the golden statue that you have set up (Dan 3:16-18).

The book of Daniel highlights the contrast between YHWH and the powerless gods, thereby reflecting the same polemic against foreign gods of the writing prophets.[7]

SELF-ASSURANCE AND SELF-CRITICISM

Similar to the books of Ecclesiastes and Lamentations, the book of Job is not dedicated to the defense of faith against the outside, but rather to self-assurance of the pious when faith is challenged by suffering and the futility of life. In particular, it investigates the question of wise behavior under difficult circumstances. The book of Job reflects on personal thoughts in an apologetic situation, and thereby fathoms the possibilities and limits of apologetics, for example, from an ethical perspective. The three friends of Job are accused of moral obliquity in respect to their "apologetics." In their enthusiasm of defending God's greatness, they cross the border between truth and lie. Today this approach could be called *pia fraus*, "pious fraud": "Will you speak falsely for God, and speak deceitfully for him? . . . He will surely rebuke you" (Job 13:7, 10).

BENEFIT OF BELIEF IN GOD

Wisdom apologetics leads back to the existential question of whether it makes sense at all to believe in God. Even if the existence of God is not questioned, his justice, power, or ability to hear and see the believer and his situation may also come into question. Doubts occur not only within the believer's mindset but also through the arguments of disputing opponents.[8]

---

7. Gladd, *Revealing Mysterion*, 47, n. 136, against Goldingay, *Daniel*, 54. See Seow, "Mountain," 359, n. 18 with further references.

8. Therefore, some of the arguments presented here must be taken up once more in the following chapter, "Citatory Apologetics as Antithetic Proclamation."

The question of benefit is more than a modern superficial consideration (i.e., which religious system best serves one's own selfish attitude). On the contrary, the question of benefit tackles the matter of devotion: Does God deserve one's total surrender; is he really a trustworthy and faithful foundation for life?

Prophetic Background

We cannot expect theoretically established forms of modern atheism to have existed in biblical times. However, the writing prophets do give witness to thought structures of "practical atheism." Mislead by a feeling of security and invulnerability, the contemporaries of Isaiah could no longer imagine a God taking notice of their evil deeds:

> You felt secure in your wickedness; you said, "No one sees me." Your wisdom and your knowledge led you astray, and you said in your heart, "I am, and there is no one besides me" (Isa 47:10, 30:15–16).

This attitude is not restricted to times of prosperity. In bad times people can also have the feeling that the existence of God makes no difference in their lives:

> It is vain to serve God. What do we profit by keeping his command or by going about as mourners before the LORD of hosts? 15 Now we count the arrogant happy; evildoers not only prosper, but when they put God to the test they escape (Mal 3:14–15; Jer 18:12).

Here, too, the argument starts with a denial of God's perceptive faculties, as can be seen in the fatalistic sayings preserved by Jeremiah and Ezekiel:

> How long will the land mourn, and the grass of every field wither? For the wickedness of those who live in it the animals and the birds are swept away, and because people said, "He is blind to our ways" (Jer 12:4).

Two times Ezekiel cites an obviously popular proverb of his time: "The LORD does not see us, the LORD has forsaken the land" (Ezek 8:12, 9:9). As in the polemic against idols, not only the deity's ability to perceive is questioned, but also the ability to act. This includes the act of punishment:

> He will do nothing. No evil will come upon us, and we shall not see sword or famine (Jer 5:12, Hos 10:3).

This also acts of blessing and grace: "The LORD will not do good, nor will he do harm" (Zeph 1:12). Some people are so convinced of the inefficiency of God that they dare to challenge his wrath: "Where is the LORD your God?" (Mic 7:10, Jer 17:15).

Even if God would be able to act, his present deeds did not coincide with the revelation of his character attributes: "The way of the lord [hebr. *ădōnāy*] is unfair" (Ezek 18:25, 29). In analogy to the modern question of theodicy, the ancient people were quick to understand that the tie between the power and goodness of God is hard to accept in the context of personal or collective experiences of inequity and suffering.

There is just one step from the cry for God's intervening justice—"Where is the God of justice?" (Mal 2:17)—to the accusing despair of the disappointed: "Where is the LORD your God?" (Mic 7:10, Joel 2:17).

Psalm 10

In the wisdom canon, Psalm 10 reiterates three deliberations of the wicked.[9] They question God's faculty of perception (v. 11), his mere existence (v. 4), and the consequences of their deeds (v. 6):

> In the pride of their countenance the wicked say, "God will not seek it out"; all their thoughts are, "There is no God." . . . They think in their heart, "We shall not be moved; throughout all generations we shall not meet adversity." . . . They think in their heart, "God has

---

9. Psalms 9 and 10 are generally understood as a unit because of their joint acrostic structure.

forgotten, he has hidden his face, he will never see it" (Ps 10:4, 6, 11).

These thoughts are not without effect to the Psalmist, who also feels the absence of God in light of the observed situation: "Why, O LORD, do you stand far off? Why do you hide yourself in times of trouble?" (v. 1). However, the Psalmist abstains from drawing a direct correlation between the seemingly passivity of YHWH and the activity of the wicked.[10]

Perspective of the Oppressed and their Spectators

Since life experience seems to disprove his faith, the oppressed suffers discouragement by the sometimes well-intended, sometimes cynical and contemptuous advice of his contemporaries:

> All who see me mock at me; they make mouths at me, they shake their heads; "Commit your cause to the LORD; let him deliver—let him rescue the one in whom he delights!" (Ps 22:8–9 [7–8]).

The question of the spectators "Where is Your God" (42:4, 11 [3, 10]) can quickly turn into the verdict "There is no help for you in God" (Ps 3:3 [2]). This question—referring to the individual sufferer—is related to the same question on a collective, national level: "Why should the nations say, 'Where is their God?'" (Pss 79:10, 115:2). This question of the worldwide reputation of YHWH is a concern that leads back to the exodus event and Deut 9:28.[11]

Perspective of the Wicked

The wicked in the book of Psalms can defend their position by looking at the miserable lives of the righteous. Usually, however, they argue from their own unhindered evildoing. Just as in the

---

10. Sager, *Polyphonie des Elends*, 123, referring to Job 9:24 with a stronger urge towards accusation.

11. See above, n. 126 for further references.

writing prophets, they too question the perceptive faculties of YHWH: "Who ... will hear us?" (Ps 59:8 [7]). "Who can see us?" (64:6–7 [5–6], 94:7), and more generally: "How can God know?" (73:11). Using pictoral language, Eliphaz accuses Job of just such an attitude:

> Therefore you say, "What does God know? Can he judge through the deep darkness? Thick clouds enwrap him, so that he does not see, and he walks on the dome of heaven" (Job 22:13–14).

In the same context, Eliphaz accuses the wicked in general of denying God's ability to act (even if he would perceive something): "They said to God, 'Leave us alone,' and 'What can the Almighty do to us?'" (v. 17).

Increase of Prosperity

The expression *sûr mimmennû*, "Leave us alone," refers back to Job 21:14 (cf. Isa 30:11, using different words), where the wicked are quoted with the words:[12]

> Leave us alone! We do not desire to know your ways. What is the Almighty, that we should serve him? And what profit do we get if we pray to him? (Job 21:14–15).

The calculation of benefit, as demonstrated here (also in Mal 3:14–15), can reassure the wicked and alienate the righteous. Two times Elihu puts this idea into Job's mouth, once as a question, once as a statement:

> If you ask, "What advantage have I? How am I better off than if I had sinned?" (Job 35:3).

> For he has said, "It profits one nothing to take delight in God" (34:9).

---

12. The question *mah-šadday*, "What is the Almighty?," leads back to the Pharaoh's answer in Exodus 5:2: *mî YHWH*, "Who is the LORD [that I should heed him]," which is taken up in the wisdom canon in Proverbs 30:9. As we have seen, it plays a decisive role in the apologetic controversy of the book of Exodus.

Job is accused of denying that belief in God makes any sense. Georg Fohrer makes a connection between this calculation, which eventually leads to faithlessness, and the theological root of the piety of Job's friends. The,y as well, first ask about their benefit and then decide if it is better to stand on God's side.

> It is remarkable that Job ascribes to the wicked the same reasoning for their wickedness, which both Satan (1:9) and the friends (5:8, 8:5, 11:13, especially 12:2) attribute as the root of piety. Its use can lead to wickedness, just as easily as to disconcerting piety.[13]

Moral Benefit

It is interesting to observe how those, who deny the potent existence of God in their life, are labeled *rāšāʿ* ,"wicked," and *nābāl*,"fool," (Pss 10:4, 14:1, 53:2). For the Old Testament, there is a natural connection between the fear of God and morality, as well as wisdom. The argument behind this can easily be understood with the help of a practical example provided by Job:

> The eye of the adulterer also waits for the twilight, saying, "No eye will see me"; and he disguises his face (Job 24:15).

The adulterer has ultimately blotted out the existence, the perceptual ability or at least the retributive justice of God: "No eye—and we can add: even not God's eye—will see me." Practical atheism and sinfulness promote each other.

Intellectual Benefit

On the background of the Mosaic law, the moral benefit of belief in God is self-evident. On an intellectual level, the practical unbeliever usually feels superior and self-secure: He seems to see through the slavish faith of the righteous, and gains success from

---

13. Fohrer, *Hiob*, 343, my translation.

his footloose and fancy-free ways of decision-making (Prov 12:15, 26:12).

In contrast to that epistemological approach, the books of Job and Proverbs defend the thesis that the fear of God does not hinder, but promote, and even presuppose, an increase in knowledge.

> The fear of the LORD is instruction in wisdom, and
> humility goes before honor
> (Prov 15:33, 1:7, 9:10, Job 28:28).

With "wisdom," the benefit of godliness reaches beyond the intellectual dimension. Wisdom in the book of Proverbs is a "*life*-skill: the ability of the individual to conduct his life in the best possible way and to the best possible effect."[14] The wise person is able to conduct his life for the benefit of himself, his neighbor, and for the glory of God.[15]

The definition of wisdom as "an intellectual quality that provides the key to happiness and success, to 'life' in its widest sense"[16] indicates that from a long-term lifetime perspective, the cost-benefit-analysis of the wicked is going to fail. In the long run, the wisdom gained by the fear of God provides fulfillment in life. Assessed from the absoluteness of God's point of view, the life of the righteous reaches its target.

---

14. Whybray, *Proverbs*, 4, quoted in Lucas, "Wisdom Theology," 902. See the term *Lebenskunst*, "life-skill," used by Hermisson, "Weisheit," 200.

15. For these three dimensions, Steinberg, "Gottes Ordnungen," 211, referring to Frydrych, *Living Under the Sun*, 18, 52, 80.

16. Whybray, *Intellectual Tradition*, 8, quoted in Lucas, "Wisdom Theology," 902.

7

Citatory Apologetics as Antithetic Proclamation

A REMARKABLE PHENOMENON WITHIN the Old Testament is the frequent quotation of deviating opinions, not in order to point out commonalities, but to build up contradictions. In his investigation on the more than 250 records of such quotations in the later prophets, Hans Walter Wolff calls this phenomenon "antithetic proclamation" *(antithetische Verkündigung)*.[1]

In his genre study, Adrian Graffy provides a survey of the history of research on the formal aspect of the phenomenon. From the outset, he draws back to Hermann Gunkel's category of disputation *(Streitgespräch, Disputation)*.[2] Graffy rejects Claus Westermann's suggestion to replace the term "disputation" by the term *Bestreitung,* "contest," when the dialogue is not presented in direct speech, but only reported by the prophet. Graffy instead prefers to use the term "[dialogue] disputation" *(Streitgespräch, Disputation)* for the dialogue, and "disputation speech" *(Disputationswort),* when only the prophet speaks and reports

---

1. Wolff, *Zitat im Prophetenspruch,* 36–129.

2. Graffy, *Prophet Confronts,* 2–6, referring to the third part, "Die Propheten als Schriftsteller und Dichter," (xxxiv-lxx) of Gunkel, "Einleitungen," introduction to Schmidt, *Propheten,* lxvii.

the opposing viewpoint.³ A further suggestion to use the term *Diskussionswort* (which could be translated as "word of discussion" or "discussion speech") for the latter is made by Hans-Jürgen Hermisson and Klaus Koch.⁴

In part two of his study, Graffy restricts the category "disputation speech" in a strict sense to only a limited amount of biblical passages,⁵ after having filtered out "many texts . . . unworthy of" this designation:⁶

1. He finds a great number of texts, where the quotations are not given in order to be refuted, but as an illustration of the guilt of the people (e.g., Isa 22:13b, 28:9–10, 30:16).

2. Texts like Amos 5:18–20 could be called "implicit disputation speech," since the opinion of the people is not explicitly stated.

3. There are texts with an argumentative tone, which is present in other genres, such as the parables in Isaiah 5:1–7, 28:23–29, and the trial speeches in the later chapters of the book.

4. A logical sequence of thought is not necessarily a dispute, as long as there is no clear disagreement.

5. "Disputation dialogues," where each party that speaks (as we see in the book of Job) forms its own category.

6. The speeches of Malachi are not primarily intended to reject the opponents' quoted opinions. The opponents themselves

---

3. Graffy, *Prophet Confronts*, 9, referring to Westermann, "Sprache und Struktur," 124–34, reprint as Westermann and Richter, *Sprache und Struktur*, and more general, Westermann, *Grundformen*.

4. Hermisson, "Diskussionsworte," 665–80, quoted in Graffy, *Prophet Confronts*, 10; see Koch, *Amos*, 128–31, 134–35, 232–33, quoted in Graffy, *Prophet Confronts*, 18.

5. Isa 28:14–19, 40:27–31, 49:14–25; Jer 8:8–9, 31:29–30, 33:23–26; Ezek 11:2–12, 14–17, 12:21–25, 26–28, 18:1–20, 20:32–44, 33:10–20, 23–29, 37:11b–13; Hag 1:2, 4–11; Graffy, *Prophet Confronts*, 24–104.

6. Graffy, *Prophet Confronts*, 22. The eight categories are described on p. 22–23.

are only reacting to an initial statement by God. Both Malachi and his opponents are referring to this word of God.
7. For speeches beginning with *hôy*, "woe [to]," the element of threat constitutes a new category.
8. Sometimes the sequence quotation-refutation does not form a self-contained unit, but is intrinsically tied to a greater text corpus (e.g., Jer 2:23a as part of the poem Jer 2). This also cannot be called an autonomous disputation speech in a strict sense.

The formal genre of disputation together with these eight categories of Graffy provides clarification to the comprehensive amount of eligible texts. In a comprehensive canonical study however, form and genre constitute only one criterion for the classification of the material. As one of five main forms of apologetic strategy in the Old Testament, "citatory pologetics" cannot be restricted to a certain genre. It has to cover the entire thematic spectrum of defense against verbally quoted claims or counter-arguments.[7]

ROOTS OF CITATORY APOLOGETICS IN THE TORAH

From a canonical perspective, the origin of this theme-line can be traced back to the Torah. The roots can be found in the "archheretical" quote of the snake in the garden:

> Did God say, "You shall not eat from any tree in the garden"? . . . You will not die; for God knows that when you eat of it your eyes will be opened, and you will be like God, knowing good and evil (Gen 3:1, 4–5).

The context points out the deception and temptation of these words. The woman corrects the word "any," but nevertheless is trapped after focusing on what is offered here.

---

7. Only category (4) of Graffy has to be sorted out here, since there has to be an articulate contrary opinion.

Within primeval history, there are two more quotations of obviously misleading mottos. Cain's famous rhetorical question "Am I my brother's keeper?" (Gen 4:9) is intended to refute his responsibility towards his fellow human being. As already indicated, the motto of the builders of Babel (11:4) is frustrated by the course of events and the subsequent vocation of Abraham.[8]

The book of Exodus provides examples of the steady complaining of the people in the wilderness:

> Was it because there were no graves in Egypt that you have taken us away to die in the wilderness? What have you done to us, bringing us out of Egypt? Is this not the very thing we told you in Egypt, "Let us alone and let us serve the Egyptians"? For it would have been better for us to serve the Egyptians than to die in the wilderness (Exod 14:11–12).

The skillfully implemented quotation in the quotation refers back to the complaining in Egypt. The Israelites want to be slaves and accuse God of killing them by letting them starve of hunger (Exod 16:3) and thirst (17:3). At the golden calf (32:12, Deut 9:28) and after the return of the spies (Num 14:16), the same motif—a deity killing its nation—is used as argument to prevent God from extinguishing his own people (more generally, Deut 32:27). Since the enemies might not be informed about righteousness of God's judgment, they might misunderstand the demise as a hint to divine weakness.[9]

Already in the book of Exodus, the question of provision is replaced by the even more basic question of God's presence among his people: "Is the LORD among us or not?" (Exod 17:7). In the book of Psalms the question of provision is expressed in a more poetical form:

> They spoke against God, saying, "Can God spread a table in the wilderness? Even though he struck the rock so that water gushed out and torrents overflowed, can

---

8. See chapter 4, "Dispute with Human Hubris (Primeval History)."

9. See chapter 4, "YHWH and the Demise of his People—Theological Models for the Interpretation of History."

he also give bread, or provide meat for his people?" (Pss 78:19–20).

Further quotations in the book of Deuteronomy reveal fear of enemies and doubts in God's support during conquest: "These nations are more numerous than I; how can I dispossess them?" (Deut 7:17). "Who can stand up to the Anakim?" (9:2).

To the expressions of mistrust and fear, the book of Deuteronomy adds further quotations brining to light an unfaithful attitude of heart. In the land of Canaan, the people of God might develop a particular interest in the religious heritage of the ingenious population:

> take care that you are not snared into imitating them, after they have been destroyed before you: do not inquire concerning their gods, saying, "How did these nations worship their gods? I also want to do the same" (Deut 12:30).

One example is given of the "mean thought" to undermine the general thrust of compassion in the social laws, while still keeping to their wording. The approaching year of remission—"The seventh year, the year of remission, is near" (Deut 15:9)—should never lead to deliberate failure to render assistance.

A further aspect of unfaithfulness is brought up with the quotation: "We are safe even though we go our own stubborn ways" (Deut 29:19). When curse and announced disasters are not taken serious, God is not present, attentive, or capable of fulfilling his oath. As we have already seen, the background for such a saying is an attitude of "practical atheism."[10]

These thoughts occur with ever increasing frequency in quotations in the writing prophets, the book of Job, and the Psalter. In his investigation on the theology of those quotations in the writing prophets and further texts,[11] James Crenshaw detects six theologi-

10. See chapter 6, "Benefit of Belief in God."

11. Crenshaw, *Prophetic Conflict*, 23–38, focuses on the writing prophets. Furthermore he takes account of the verses: Deut 1:27, 4:6, 9:28, 12:30, 15:9, 29:19, 31:17–18; Pss 10:11, 14:1, 35:21, 25, 59:8 [7], 71:11, 73:11, 78:19–20, 94:7, 137:3, 7, 139:11–12.

cal emphases: (1) confidence in God's faithfulness (taking it for granted, irrespective of Israel's behavior), (2) satisfaction with traditional religion, (3) defiance, (4) hopelessness, (5) doubt as to God's justice, and (6) historical pragrmatism. Due to the theological continuity and interconnectedness of thought-patterns, these six categories (with slight adaption) still do justice to the extended corpus of Old Testament texts in total.

TREACHEROUS CONFIDENCE

As already observed with Psalm 10, quite a number of quotations are based on treacherous confidence of the evildoer, who is convinced that God will not interfere.[12] The righteous, on the contrary, prays and looks ahead, trusting in God's intervention.

Even if the evildoer is aware of God's presence, God's ability to see the malpractice, God's ability to interfere, and God's willingness to act in righteousness, he carries on, confident that God will not stand against him simply because he belongs to the chosen people. Jeremiah, for example, reports the false conclusion of those who deduce from the temporary silence of God that their wickedness indeed must be justified before his ethical standards:

> Also on your skirts is found the lifeblood of the innocent poor, though you did not catch them breaking in. Yet in spite of all these things you say, "I am innocent; surely his anger has turned from me." Now I am bringing you to judgment for saying, "I have not sinned" (Jer 2:34–35).

Some people are not willing to accept the severity of God's judgment. When Jeremiah announces a military attack from the North, they do not believe that there is more to their covenant with God than talking themselves into having a good conscience: "He will do nothing. No evil will come upon us, and we shall not see sword or famine" (Jer 5:12).

12. Pss 10:4, 6, 11, 14:1, 59:8, 64:6–7 [5–6], 73:11, 79:10, 94:7, 115:2; Job 24:15; Jer 5:12, 12:4, 29:15; Ezek 8:12, 9:9; Mic 2:6, 7:10; Zeph 1:12. Many of these quotations are already dealt with in the chapter 6, "Benefit of Belief in God."

Others are not willing to accept the imminence of the judgment. The story of Isaiah and Hezekiah teaches that the judgment of God might come about many years later. Hezekiah receives a specific prophetic word, on which he builds his selfish composure (2 Kgs 20:19). Many Israelites however seem to base their treacherous, misplaced confidence only on common experience: "Evil shall not overtake or meet us" (Amos 9:10). Ezekiel gives accounts of proverbs in Israel, which indicate how prevailing such an expectation has become. His answer reassures them of the imminence of what is about to happen:

> Mortal, what is this proverb of yours about the land of Israel, which says, "The days are prolonged, and every vision comes to nothing"? Tell them therefore, "Thus says the Lord GOD: I will put an end to this proverb, and they shall use it no more as a proverb in Israel." But say to them, The days are near, and the fulfillment of every vision.... Mortal, the house of Israel is saying, "The vision that he sees is for many years ahead; he prophesies for distant times." Therefore say to them, Thus says the Lord GOD: None of my words will be delayed any longer, but the word that I speak will be fulfilled, says the Lord GOD (Ezek 12:22–23, 27–28).

A huge problem is the presence of false prophets reassuring sinners of their ways. Their message can be summed up with the comforting words, "peace, peace" (Jer 6:14, 8:11). They can draw back to words of solace spoken by the prophet Isaiah and others (Isa 57:19, 1 Chr 12:18). However, they twist the words and pervert the message:

> They keep saying to those who despise the word of the LORD, "It shall be well with you"; and to all who stubbornly follow their own stubborn hearts, they say, "No calamity shall come upon you" (Jer 23:17).

In the concrete case of the Babylonian threat, this general pacification turns into specific promises. Jeremiah provides the most elaborate example of such a promise, quoting the false prophet Hananiah from Gibeon:

> Thus says the LORD of hosts, the God of Israel: I have broken the yoke of the king of Babylon. Within two years I will bring back to this place all the vessels of the LORD's house, which King Nebuchadnezzar of Babylon took away from this place and carried to Babylon. I will also bring back to this place King Jeconiah son of Jehoiakim of Judah, and all the exiles from Judah who went to Babylon, says the LORD, for I will break the yoke of the king of Babylon (Jer 28:2–4, v.11, 27:9, 14, 16).

In the background of this argument stands a twisted comprehension of election.

> Israel is YHWH's elected people that will be led to a salvific destination; Jerusalem and the temple on Zion are the inviolable places of the presence and salvific work of God; even if judgments befall the city of God—they will not overcome the holy city, and the holy remnant of Israel will rise victorious from all catastrophes. This theology carries and inspires the prophetic faith of Hananiah.[13]

The question of election stands in the background of three promises of Hananiah:

- Not the Babylonians, but the Israelites are the chosen people: Babylon will fail; the exiles will return.
- God has chosen the royal offspring of king David. Jeconiah will be brought back.
- God has chosen the house of the temple. The vessels will return.

Jeremiah could agree to the general promises, given to the elected people: The Babylonian hegemony is limited. This is not the end of temple and king. Eventually the exiles will return. However, now is the time to obey God's command and serve Nebuchadnezzar (27:11–12).[14]

---

13. Kraus, *Prophetie*, 90, my translation.
14. See Keown et al., *Jeremiah 26–52*, 54.

The election of the temple is an argument not only for Hananiah:

> Do not trust in these deceptive words: "This is the temple of the LORD, the temple of the LORD, the temple of the LORD.... We are safe!" (Jer 7:4, 10).

The trust in God's promises concerning the temple can be narrowed down to the holy of holies: "The ark of the covenant of the LORD" (Jer 3:6). It also can be widened to a trust in the protection of "Zion," the temple mountain, and the city of Jerusalem, in general. The expression *māqôm hazzeh*, "this place," clearly refers to the temple (Jer 7:3, 6–7, 20; 1 Kgs 8:29–35), but does not exclude the holy city surrounding it:

> Here are the prophets saying to them, "You shall not see the sword, nor shall you have famine, but I will give you true peace in this place" (Jer 14:13).

Jeremiah's opponents are proclaiming that the perception of Zion as indestructible is not an indication of faithlessness, but of trust in God's promises: "Who can come down against us, or who can enter our places of refuge?" (Jer 21:13). The false prophets do not preach to trust in bricks and stones. They are able to argue with spiritual matters. YHWH has provided his chosen people of Israel with his Torah and his wisdom. How can they ever stumble with these gifts? Jeremiah has to expose their baseness. What remains of that gift, if it is abused for selfish matters?

> Even the stork in the heavens knows its times; and the turtledove, swallow, and crane observe the time of their coming; but my people do not know the ordinance of the LORD. How can you say, "We are wise, and the law of the LORD is with us," when, in fact, the false pen of the scribes has made it into a lie? The wise shall be put to shame, they shall be dismayed and taken; since they have rejected the word of the LORD, what wisdom is in them? (Jer 8:7–9).

If they are paid well, the prophets do not shrink back to argue with the heart of the matter from a spiritual perspective. When it is not the building of God and not the law of God, then it is his presence, God himself, who guarantees the safety of the place of his dwelling:

> Its rulers give judgment for a bribe, its priests teach for a price, its prophets give oracles for money; yet they lean upon the LORD and say, "Surely the LORD is with us! No harm shall come upon us" (Mic 3:11).

The prophet Amos takes up the argument of election and turns it against the people (*retorsio argumenti*). They have the privilege of election. But this privilege goes together with a special responsibility and accountability. The result is not lenient favoritism but relentless pursuit of their sins:

> You only have I known of all the families of the earth;
> therefore I will punish you for all your iniquities (Amos 3:2).

SATISFACTION WITH THE STATUS QUO

A spiritual lethargy becomes noticeable, when king Ahaz of Judah evades the invitation from his living God with seemingly pious words: "I will not ask, and I will not put the LORD to the test" (Isa 7:12). His successor Hezekiah is content that the judgment will not come during his lifetime: "Why not, if there will be peace and security in my days?" (39:8; Ezek 12:22, 27).

The people of God are in deep sleep (Isa 29:10), blind (v. 9), and cannot read what is revealed to them by God: "We cannot read" (v. 12, v. 11). Does God not lose control here over his own people? Is it not a sign of weakness, if his means of communication are blocked?

Isaiah defends the honor of YHWH by explaining that God himself is the reason for that blindness:

> For the LORD has poured out upon you a spirit of deep sleep; he has closed your eyes, you prophets, and covered your heads, you seers (Isa 29:10).

God will do "amazing things" and makes foolish the wisdom of the arrogant (v.14).

The prophet himself is perceived as disruptive factor in this atmosphere of self-confident laxity. King Ahab of Israel is annoyed by the prophet Micahiah, son of Imlah: "I hate him, for he never prophesies anything favorable about me, but only disaster" (2 Kgs 22:8). Shemaiah of Nehelam labels Jeremiah as "madman who plays the prophet" and who needs to be put "in the stocks and the collar" (Jer 26:26–27). When Jehu wants to conceal his secret anointment as future king by a companion of Elisha, he can refer to this cliché and expect his audience to endorse to it:

> When Jehu came back to his master's officers, they said to him, "Is everything all right? Why did that madman come to you?" He answered them, "You know the sort and how they babble" (2 Kgs 9:11).

The prophet Hosea reports a similar denouncement: "The prophet is a fool, the man of the spirit is mad!" However, he is not willing to take that reproach and understands to counter: "Because of your great iniquity, your hostility is great" (Hos 9:7). They get what they deserve. A fool announcing insane judgments is the natural answer to a foolish people that sins like mad.

DEFIANT REFUSAL TO LISTEN

Some quotations give a strong impression of the head wind the prophets have to face: "Where is the word of the LORD? Let it come!" (Jer 17:15; Mic 7:10). Even friendly, inviting words encounter the stubborn refusal of the people to walk in the good paths ("We will not walk in it," Jer 6:16), or to listen ("I will not listen," 22:21, 6:17). They are decided not to return to YHWH again: "We are free, we will come to you no more" (Jer 2:31). The prophet's efforts are discouraged not only indirectly by their listeners' apathy, but also directly by their words:

> It is no use! We will follow our own plans, and each of us will act according to the stubbornness of our evil will (Jer 18:12).

The arrogance of the people seems to be unimpressed even by the first blows of the arriving wrath of God:

> The bricks have fallen, but we will build with dressed stones; the sycamores have been cut down, but we will put cedars in their place (Isa 9:9).

Nothing seems to be able to break the barriers of pride:

> We have made a covenant with death, and with Sheol we have an agreement; when the overwhelming scourge passes through it will not come to us; for we have made lies our refuge, and in falsehood we have taken shelter (Isa 28:15).

The prophet reacts with the proclamation that the wrath of God will not give in either: "For all this his anger has not turned away; his hand is stretched out still" (Isa 9:20, vv. 11, 16).

A defiant aversion against the word of God can as well be read from the attempts to denounce, ridicule, and muzzle the prophet:

> For I hear many whispering: "Terror is all around! Denounce him! Let us denounce him!" All my close friends are watching for me to stumble. "Perhaps he can be enticed, and we can prevail against him, and take our revenge on him" (Jer 20:10).

The prophet overcomes this irritation and finds his way back to an attitude of worship by trusting in the salvation of God (vv. 11–13). Nevertheless, he also reports how he quarrels with his fate and with God (vv. 14–18).

Isaiah takes up the accusations of a childish, incomprehensible message and reformulates it as a word of judgment:

> "Whom will he teach knowledge, and to whom will he explain the message? Those who are weaned from milk, those taken from the breast? For it is precept upon

> precept, precept upon precept, line upon line, line upon line, here a little, there a little."
>
> Truly, with stammering lip and with alien tongue he will speak to this people, to whom he has said, "This is rest; give rest to the weary; and this is repose"; yet they would not hear. Therefore the word of the LORD will be to them, "Precept upon precept, precept upon precept, line upon line, line upon line, here a little, there a little;" in order that they may go, and fall backward, and be broken, and snared, and taken (Isa 28:9–13).

The people do not want to hear painful messages. Prophetic words like these are forbidden or twisted:

> For they are a rebellious people, faithless children, children who will not hear the instruction of the LORD; who say to the seers, "Do not see"; and to the prophets, "Do not prophesy to us what is right; speak to us smooth things, prophesy illusions, leave the way, turn aside from the path, let us hear no more about the Holy One of Israel" (Isa 30:9–11; Jer 11:19, 21).

The new parole then is: "It shall be well with you . . . No calamity shall come upon you" (Jer 23:17). This is proclaimed with the authority of "I have dreamed" (v. 25), "says the LORD" (v. 31, Ezek 13:2) or as would-be, "burden of the LORD" (vv. 34, 38).

This leads to situations where prophetic oracle stands against prophetic oracle, accusation against accusation (Jer 23:9–40). When both prophets accuse each other of apostasy and sinful behavior, it becomes more and more difficult to decide who is right and who is wrong. The above-mentioned criterion of moral offenses[15] can no longer lead to clarification. Therefore, in his dispute in chapter 28, the prophet Jeremiah pursues a different strategy and expresses his wish that the deceitful promise of salvation by Hananiah should become true:

> Amen! May the LORD do so; may the LORD fulfill the words that you have prophesied (Jer 23:6).

---

15. See chapter 5, "Moral Offenses by the Representatives."

Jeremiah makes his point that he does not begrudge the people the fulfillment of a promise. However, he modestly dares to add, a promise does not become true by its articulation, but by its fulfillment (v. 9). Jeremiah makes these statements with the (sad) certainty that God will, in the end, confirm his own prophecy and belie his wish and Hananiah's prophecy (v. 17).

HOPELESSNESS

When YHWH courts Israel like a bridegroom his unfaithful bride, the verdict of the people on this relationship is *nô'āš*, "it is hopeless"—because "I have loved strangers, and after them I will go" (Jer 2:25, 18:12).

The fear of God does not seem to pay off; the oracles of the prophets do not seem to come true. Therefore, people bet on other horses. They put their trust in other gods and federations with mighty nations:

> For thus said the Lord GOD, the Holy One of Israel: In returning and rest you shall be saved; in quietness and in trust shall be your strength. But you refused and said, "No! We will flee upon horses"—therefore you shall flee! and, "We will ride upon swift steeds"—therefore your pursuers shall be swift! (Isa 30:15–16).

DOUBTS IN GOD'S JUSTICE AND POWER

Doubts in God's justice and power are expressed in many parts of the Hebrew Bible (Genesis 18, Exodus 32, the book of Job, and Habakkuk),[16] however not always treated by means of citatory apologetics.

One positive example of antithetic proclamation is the prophet Ezekiel, who deals extensively in chapter 18 of his book with the allegation: "The way of the Lord is unfair" (vv. 25, 29),

---

16. Crenshaw, *Prophetic Conflict*, 30; Westermann, *Lob und Klage*, 146; Wolff, *Zitat im Prophetenspruch*, 100–1; Ramm, "Apologetic," 15–16.

expressed in the proverb: "The parents have eaten sour grapes, and the children's teeth are set on edge" (v.2, Jer 31:29–30; Lam 5:7). Ezekiel comes up with first ideas of a distinction between God's will and God's permission:

> Have I any pleasure in the death of the wicked, says the Lord GOD, and not rather that they should turn from their ways and live? (Ezek 18:23, 32).

The prophet Malachi has to face similar questions:

> You have wearied the LORD . . . By saying, "All who do evil are good in the sight of the LORD, and he delights in them." Or by asking, "Where is the God of justice?" (Mal 2:17; Jer 5:19).

Malachi reacts with the announcement of a swift judgment and justifies the decision made by God by giving evidence of several offenses.

HISTORICAL PRAGMATISM

The considerations about the "queen of heaven" in Jeremiah 44:16–19, which have been dealt with already in relation to their particular interpretation of history,[17] reveal beyond that an attitude of choosing one's religion according to considerations of practical benefit. When YHWH wants to win over the obedience of his people, it has to pay off for them, and this as quickly as possible.

> Let him make haste, let him speed his work that we may see it; let the plan of the Holy One of Israel hasten to fulfillment, that we may know it!" (Isa 5:19).

But how can the people ever be sure that they really have fulfilled their part of the deal? The prophet Haggai uncovers the weakness of such pragmatic considerations. Yes, "You have looked for much, and, lo, it came to little" (Hag 1:9). The meager benefits of their covenant relationship do not point to a negligent covenant deity,

---

17. See chapter 4, "YHWH and the Demise of his People—Theological Models for the Interpretation of History."

but to a negligent covenant people (vv. 5–11). Pragmatic conclusions have to be drawn very carefully. Without prophetic authority the lessons from history always stay ambivalent.[18]

---

18. Crenshaw, *Prophetic Conflict*, 31–32.

8

Exemplary Apologetics
Case Learning

IT MIGHT NOT BE the number of apologetic disputes, but the scope of texts treating them, which might surprise the reader of the Old Testament. In some instances, the apologetic dialogues and monologues range over several chapters. The ten plagues in Egypt with the purpose to communicate knowledge of God are accompanied by a comprehensive portrayal of the dispute between Moses and the Pharaoh (Exod 5–12). The judge Jephthah defends the legitimacy of the conquest of Canaan by Israel against tenures of the Ammonites (Judg 11:12–27). David defends God's honor against Goliath not only with a slingshot, but also with arguments (1 Sam 17:43–47). The miracle at Mount Carmel is accompanied with arguments of Elisha before the people, including his ridicule of the Baal priests (1 Kgs 18:21–37).[1] The taunting by Rabshakeh is reported at length, followed by a word of God, a further speech of Rabshakeh, a prayer, and a further word of God (2 Kgs 18–19; Isa 36–37). The dispute between Jeremiah and Hananiah is decided by the death of the false prophet (Jer 28). The first six chapters of the book of Daniel exemplify in form of a dialogue the apology

---

1. Preuß, *Verspottung*, 80–100.

of Israelite religion (dietary rules, exclusive worship of God) in front of the rulers of the world. The debates with opponents of the post-exilic temple and wall building projects are documented in the book Ezra-Nehemiah by quotations, letters, and prayers.[2]

How should we understand this notable phenomenon of detailed reports of individual conversations and defense speeches? Obviously, these texts do not serve the purpose of documenting a comprehensive defense of Israelite religion. Such an idea can not be substantiated in the intellectual history of the Hebrew Bible. In fact the purpose of these texts can be seen in the reassurance of the reader's faith. Furthermore, the reader is provided with arguments, illustrations, and examples for the defense of his beliefs. From a didactic point of view we can describe these texts as samples, intentionally designed to encourage the reader to take up the dialogue with dissenting opponents.

There is a focus on three groups of potential dialogue partners:

- Military opponents
  (Goliath, Rabshakeh, the opponents of the wall-building project)
- Religious representatives of other faith groups
  (gentile priests, false prophets)
- The powerful and the rulers of other nations
  (rulers of the Egyptians, Ammonites, Assyrians, Babylonians, Medo-Persians)

The third group is of special interest for the theological orientation of the texts. The reader is encouraged not to shy away from political authorities.

A decisive impact on the fate and fortunes of the people of Israel is ascribed to the influence of individuals on the hearts of the powerful of this world.

---

2. Ezra 4:2-5, 8-22, 5:3-4, 7-17, 6:6-12, 7:12-26; Neh 2:19-20, 3:33-38, 6:1-14.

9

Apologetics as Challenge and Mandate

FURTHER QUESTIONS

THIS BRIEFLY SKETCHED OUTLINE of biblical-theological apologetics leads to further questions that cannot be treated here extensively, but should to be considered before drawing the final conclusions.

In all themes of Old Testament theology, the wisdom canon can be understood as a test case for the methodological stringency of the argument. In his concise survey of modern approaches to Old Testament theology, Gerhard Hasel observes, "Virtually all OT theologies have difficulties in dealing with the wisdom writings."[1] Here it becomes evident in how far the methodological approach is capable of doing justice to the broad diversity of the Old Testament world of faith. In the present investigation, it has been possible to draw some theological trajectories from the narrative and prophetic type of apologetics to the wisdom type. In further stud-

---

1. Hasel, *Theology*, 45–46, who refers to Gerhard von Rad, Walther Zimmerli, Claus Westermann, and particularly, Clements, *Old Testament Theology*. See Uehlinger, "Medien altorientalischer Theologien," 142, n. 6, detecting fundamental problems with Old Testament wisdom literature in the approaches of Gerhard von Rad and Horst Dietrich Preuß.

ies, it should be possible to confirm and deepen the understanding of this briefly sketched connection. Another question pertains to whether the particular formal and thematic character of texts of the third canon part can be determined in still more distinct contours, and differentiated more clearly from the remaining corpus.

Within the framework of a specific *Christian* apologetics, the question arises as to where exactly in the New Testament the located lines of argument are taken up and how they are pursued and developed. How are the presented canonical types of apologetics interpreted intrabiblically, and how are they utilized in the second part of the Christian Bible?

TOWARD A NEW APPROACH TO OLD TESTAMENT APOLOGETICS

Despite the number of not yet completely answered questions, this study uncovers a number of interconnected means and strategies, by which the authors of the Hebrew Bible face the contemporary challenges to their worldview. In the past, the focus on prophetic apologetics ("polemics") has oftentimes led to the impression that there is only one typical way to counter the attacks. Including the totality of the Hebrew canon into the scheme, however, leads to the discovery of a surprising variety and diversity. The multitude of *direct* confrontations in the form of dialogue, dispute, citation, defense speech, etc.,—in prose as well as in poetry—is accompanied by an *indirect* approach to apologetics, which comprises a considerable scope within the historical and narrative texts of the Hebrew Bible.

The terms "polemics" and "mockery" *(Verspottung)*, which have oftentimes been preferred in previous research, are not to betray the fact that the argumentation takes place on a rational level in a predominantly "nonpolemical" and factual way. The texts persuade with logic (and are intended to objectively correct what has been wrongfully alleged), pictorially illustrate, announce salvation or judgment, and demonstrate the fulfillment of prophecy in life and deeds.

INTENTIONAL IMPACT ON THE READER

During the last few decades, the comparatively young approach of speech-act theory[2] has drawn new attention of biblical interpretation to the impact of the text on the reader himself.

We cannot explain Old Testament apologetics comprehensively, as long as we restrict ourselves to merely describing the propositional content of the statements in the texts. Every propositional statement is usually connected to an "illocutionary force." (John Austin defines this force as the "performance of an act *in* saying something as opposed to performance of an act *of* saying something").[3] In the course of their apologetic reasoning, the authors intend to continuously influence and change the behavior of the readers and their relationship of challenges of their belief systems. Two examples demonstrate this clearly:

In the present study, we have noted a line of inducing arguments, which have their roots particularly in the book of Deuteronomy. If we follow the terminology of John Searle, they can be labeled as "directives." Directives are attempts "by the speaker to get the hearer to do something,"[4] using verbs like *order, command,* and *advice*.

The non-educated reader of the law is not to be excluded as a passive observer of religious debates that are too advanced for him, but urged to be proactive and take initiative. The task of defense against the intrusion of foreign religious elements is not restricted to political or religious leaders but explicitly put in the hands of the common people, the hearers, and readers of the law: "you must not heed the words of those prophets" (Deut 13:3). There is no reason

---

2. This approach has been introduced by John L. Austin in his 1955 William James Lectures at Harvard University, published 1962 as *How to Do Things with Words*.

3. Austin, *How to Do Things*, 99–100.

4. Searle, *Expression and Meaning*, 13, example verbs on p.14. For the defense of his terminology against the deviating concept of Austin, *How to Do Things*, 148–64. See also Searle, "Classification," 1–23, and the synopsis in Thiselton, *New Horizons*, 283–91.

for the "lay people" to knuckle under the "expert" in holy matters: "do not be frightened by it [or him]" (18:22).

Every male adult member of the Israelite community should "always be ready" to profess his faith (1 Pet 3:15):

> When your children ask you in time to come, "What is the meaning of the decrees and the statutes and the ordinances that the LORD our God has commanded you?" then you shall say to your children, "We were Pharaoh's slaves in Egypt, but the LORD brought us out of Egypt with a mighty hand." (Deut 6:20–25).[5]

A second example is a group of texts that can be located in the book of Psalms.[6] According to the classification system of Searle, they are to be labeled as "comissives." In these texts, the speaker commits himself "to some future course of action" with verbs such as *shall, intend, favor*, etc.,[7] "For this I will extol you, O LORD, among the nations, and sing praises to your name" (Pss 18:50 [49], 57:10 [9], 108:4 [3]). These declarations of intent cannot be understood as mere reports of the author's personal future plans. The main purpose of the poem is to be prayed repeatedly by the reader. This naturally has consequences for his attitude and conduct.

On the basis of Donald Evans' "hermeneutic of self-involvement" and the work of Richard Biggs,[8] Anthony Thiselton comments on the impact of a Psalm on its reader:

> Does it count-generate acts of renewed faith, or does it merely generate a portrayal of the Psalmist's trust? . . . It functions *as a self-involving illocutionary act, which carries practical consequences for the life and behaviour of the reader.*[9]

---

5. Exod 12:26–27, 13:14–15; Jos 4:6, 21–24.

6. See chapter 6, "Public Dispute (Doxological-Confessional)."

7. Searle, *Expression and Meaning*, 14.

8. Biggs, *Words in Action*, 147–215 (chapters 5 and 6), building on Evans, *Logic of Self-Involvement*.

9. Thiselton, *New Horizons*, 599, italics his, referring to the example of Psalm 25:2.

The impact of a liturgical prayer of intention, such as, "Then I shall have an answer for those who taunt me . . . I will also speak of your decrees before kings" (Pss 119:42, 46), is in no way inferior to the commitment expressed in the New Testament *locus classicus* of 1 Peter 3:15.

Not least of all for this reason, the Old Testament deserves a prominent place within the scope of a biblical theology of apologetics.

Bibliography

Adam, Alfred. *Die Aufgabe der Apologetik.* Leipzig: Dörffling & Franke, 1931.

Aland, Kurt. *Apologie der Apologetik: Zur Haltung und Aufgabe evangelischen Christentums in den Auseinandersetzungen der Gegenwart.* Hilfe für's Amt 15. Berlin: Christlicher Zeitschriftenverlag, 1948.

Albertz, Rainer. *Persönliche Frömmigkeit und offizielle Religion: Religionsinterner Pluralismus in Israel und Babylon.* CThM A/9. Stuttgart: Calwer 1978.

Alexander, T. Desmond. *From Paradise to the Promised Land: An Introduction to the Pentateuch,* 3rd ed. Grand Rapids: Baker, 2012.

Amit, Yairah. "Hidden Polemic in the Conquest of Dan: Judges XVII–XVIII." *VT* 60 (1990) 4–20. https://www.jstor.org/stable/1519259.

———. *Hidden Polemics in Biblical Narrative.* BIS 25. Leiden: Brill, 2000.

Ammann, Sonja. *Götter für die Toren: Die Verbindung von Götterpolemik und Weisheit im Alten Testament.* BZAW 466. Berlin: De Gruyter, 2015.

Austin, John L. *How to Do Things with Words,* 2nd ed. Cambridge, MA: Harvard University Press, 1975.

Bahnsen, Greg L. "Socrates or Christ: The Reformation of Christian Apologetics." In *Foundations of Christian Scholarship: Essays in the Van Til Perspective,* edited by Gary North, 191–267. Vallecito, CA: Ross House, 1976.

Barker, William D. *Isaiah's Kingship Polemic: An Exegetical Study in Isaiah 24–27.* FAT 2/70. Tübingen: Mohr/Siebeck, 2014.

Barnard, Leslie Willam. "Apologetik I. Alte Kirche." *TRE* 3 (1978) 371–411.

Barth, Karl. *Church Dogmatics, Volume I: The Doctrine of the Word of God. § 1–7. The Word of God as the Criterion of Dogmatics,* edited by Geoffrey William Bromiley and Thomas Forsyth Torrance. Study ed. Edinburgh: T. & T. Clark, 2010.

———. *Die Kirchliche Dogmatik. Erster Band. Die Lehre vom Wort Gottes. Erster Halbband.* Zollikon-Zürich: Evangelischer Verlag, 1952.

———. *Die Kirchliche Dogmatik. Vierter Band. Die Lehre von der Versöhnung. Dritter Teil. Erste Hälfte.* Zollikon-Zürich: Evangelischer Verlag, 1959.

———. *Die Protestantische Theologie im 19. Jahrhundert: Ihre Geschichte und ihre Vorgeschichte.* 6th ed. Zürich: TVZ, 1994.

———. *Protestant Theology in the Nineteenth Century: Its Background and History*, 3rd ed. Grand Rapids: Eerdmans, 2002.

———. *The Church Dogmatics, Volume IV: The Doctrine of Reconciliation, Part 3.2*, edited by Geoffrey William Bromiley and Thomas Forsyth Torrance. Edinburgh: T. & T. Clark, 1961.

Bauks, Michaela. *Die Welt am Anfang: Zum Verhältnis von Vorwelt und Weltentstehung in Gen 1 und in der altorientalischen Literatur*. WMANT 74. Neukirchen-Vluyn: Neukirchener, 1997.

Bayer, Oswald. *Theologie*. HST 1. Gütersloh: Gütersloher, 1994.

Beattie, Francis R. *Apologetics, or the Rational Vindication of Christianity, Volume 1: Fundamental Apologetics*. Richmond, VA: Presbyterion Committee of Publication, 1903. https://archive.org/details/apologeticsorrato1beat.

Becking, Bob. "Jeremiah 44: A Dispute on History and Religion." In *Religious Polemics in Context*, edited by Theo L. Hettema and Arie van der Kooij, 255–64. STAR 11. Assen: Van Gorcum, 2004.

Beckwith, Roger. *The Old Testament Canon of the New Testament Church and its Background in Early Judaism*. London: SPCK, 1985.

Beilby, James K. *Thinking About Christian Apologetics: What It Is and Why We Do It*. Downers Grove, IL: InterVarsity, 2011.

Beißer, Friedrich. *Der christliche Glaube: Eine Dogmatik in fünf Teilbänden, Band 1*. Neuendettelsau: Freimund, 2008.

———. "Zur Grundlegung der Apologetik." *KuD* 15 (1969) 210–25.

Berger, Klaus. *Formen und Gattungen im Neuen Testament*. Tübingen: Francke, 2005.

———. *Formgeschichte des Neuen Testaments*. Heidelberg: Quelle & Meyer, 1984.

Berkouwer, Gerrit Cornelis. *A Half Century of Theology: Movements and Motives*. Grand Rapids: Eerdmans, 1977.

Berlejung, Angelika. *Die Theologie der Bilder. Herstellung und Einweihung von Kultbildern in Mesopotamien und die alttestamentliche Bilderpolemik*. OBO 162. Freiburg: Universitätsverlag 1998.

Biggs, Richard. *Words in Action. Speech Act Theory and Biblical Interpretation*. Edinburgh: T. & T. Clark, 2001.

Birkner, Hans-Joachim. "Schleiermachers 'Kurze Darstellung' als theologisches Reformprogramm." In *Schleiermacher im besonderen Hinblick auf seine Wirkungsgeschichte in Dänemark. Vorträge des Kolloquiums am 19. und 20. November 1984*, edited by Helge Hultberg et al., 59–81. Kopenhagener Kolloquien zur deutschen Literatur 13, Text & Kontext, Sonderreihe 22. Kopenhagen: Text und Kontext, 1986. Reprint, *Schleiermacher-Studien*, edited by Hans-Joachim Birkner. Schleiermacher-Archiv 16, 285–305. Berlin: De Gruyter, 1996.

Blenkinsopp, Joseph. "The Structure of P." *CBQ* 38 (1976) 275–92. https://www.jstor.org/stable/43715146.

Blum, Erhard. *Studien zur Komposition des Pentateuch*. BZAW 189. Berlin: De Gruyter, 1990.

BIBLIOGRAPHY

Boa, Kenneth D. and Bowman, Robert M. *Faith Has Its Reasons. Integrative Approaches to Defending the Christian Faith.* Downers Grove, IL: InterVarsity, 2001.

Brandt, Peter. *Endgestalten des Kanons: das Arrangement der Schriften Israels in der jüdischen und christlichen Bibel.* BBB 131. Berlin: Philo, 2001.

Bruce, F. F. *The Apostolic Defence of the Gospel: Christian Apologetic in the New Testament.* London: InterVarsity, 1959.

Brueggemann, Walter. *Theology of the Old Testament: Testimony, Dispute, Advocacy.* Minneapolis: Fortress, 1997.

Brunner, Emil. "Die andere Aufgabe der Theologie." *Zwischen den Zeiten* 7 (1929) 255–76. Reprint, *Ein offenes Wort. Vorträge und Aufsätze 1917–1934. Band I,* edited by Rudolf Wehrli, 171–193. Zürich: TVZ, 1981.

———. *Die Mystik und das Wort: Der Gegensatz zwischen moderner Religionsauffassung und christlichem Glauben dargestellt an der Theologie Schleiermachers,* 2nd ed. Tübingen: Mohr/Siebeck, 1928.

———. *The Christian Doctrine of God: Dogmatics, vol. I.* Translated by Olive Wyon. Philadelphia: Westminster, 1950.

Bührer, Walter. *Am Anfang... Untersuchungen zur Textgenese und zur relativchronologischen Einordnung von Gen 1–3.* FRLANT 256. Göttingen: Vandenhoeck & Ruprecht, 2014.

Carnell, Edward J. *An Introduction to Christian Apologetics: A Philosophical Defense of the Trinitarian-Theistic Faith.* Grand Rapids: Eerdmans, 1948.

Carr, David M. *Reading the Fractures of Genesis: Historical and Literary Approaches.* Louisville: Westminster John Knox, 1996.

Chazan, Robert. "Apologetics I. Introduction." *EBR* 2 (2009) 414–16.

———. "Apologetics II. Judaism." *EBR* 2 (2009) 416–26.

Childs, Brevard S. *Biblical Theology of the Old and New Testament: Theological Reflections on the Christian Bible.* Minneapolis: Fortress, 1992.

Chisholm, Robert B. "The Polemic against Baalism in Israel's Early History and Literature." *BS* 150 (1994) 267–83.

Clements, Ronald E. *Old Testament Theology: A Fresh Approach.* London: Marshall, Morgan & Scott, 1978.

Clifford, Richard J. "The Function of Idol Passage in Second Isaiah." *CBQ* 42 (1980) 450–64. https://www.jstor.org/stable/43718834.

Coats, George W. *Genesis with Introduction to Narrative Literature.* FOTL 1. Grand Rapids: Eerdmans, 1983.

Cowan, Steven B. "Introduction." In *Five Views on Apologetics,* edited by Steven B. Cowan, 7–20. Grand Rapids: Zondervan, 2000.

Crenshaw, James L. *Prophetic Conflict: Its Effect Upon Israelite Religion.* BZAW 124. Berlin: De Gruyter, 1971.

Crossan, John Dominic. *The Birth of Christianity: Discovering What Happened in the Years Immediately After the Execution of Jesus.* New York, NY: Bloomsbury, 1998.

Dascal, Marcelo. "On the Uses of Argumentative Reason in Religious Polemics." In *Religious Polemics in Context*, edited by Theo L. Hettema and Arie van der Kooij, 3–20. STAR 11. Assen: Van Gorcum, 2004.

Dick, Michael Brennan. "Prophetic Parodies of Making the Cult Image." In *Born in Heaven Made on Earth. The Making of the Cult Image in the Ancient Near East*, edited by Michael Brennan Dick, 1–53. Winona Lake, IN: Eisenbrauns, 1999.

Dillmann, August. *Die Bücher Numeri, Deuteronomium und Josua*. KeH, 2nd ed. Leipzig: Hirzel, 1886. https://archive.org/details/diebchernumerioodilluoft.

Dohmen, Christoph. *Das Bilderverbot: Seine Entstehung und seine Entwicklung im Alten Testament*. BBB 620. Königstein: Hanstein, 1985.

Drey, Johann Sebastian von. *Die Apologetik als wissenschaftliche Nachweisung der Göttlichkeit des Christenthums in seiner Erscheinung, Band 1: Philosophie der Offenbarung*. Mainz: Kupferberg, 1838. https://books.google.de/books?id=-nMrAAAAYAAJ.

Droge, Arthur J. "Apologetics, NT." *ABD* 1 (1992) 302–7.

Dulles, Avery. *A History of Apologetics*. London: Hutchinson, 1971.

Dumbrell, William J. *Covenant and Creation: A Theology of the Old Testament Covenants*, 2nd ed. Carlisle: Paternoster, 2013.

Dyrness, William A. *Christian Apologetics in a World Community*. Downers Grove, IL: InterVarsity, 1983.

———. *Themes in Old Testament Theology*. Downers Grove, IL: InterVarsity Press Academic, 1977.

Emanuel, David. *From Bards to Biblical Exegesis: A Close Reading and Intertextual Analysis of Selected Exodus Psalms*. Eugene, OR: Pickwick, 2012.

Enger, Peter A. *Die Adoptivkinder Abrahams: Eine exegetische Spurensuche zur Vorgeschichte des Proselytentums*. BEATAJ 53. Frankfurt am Main: Lang, 2006.

Evans, Donald. *The Logic of Self-Involvement: A Philosophical Study of Everyday Language with Special Reference to the Christian Use of Language about God as Creator*. London: SCM, 1963.

Ferguson, Everett. "Apologetics in the New Testament," *RestQ* 6 (1962) 189–96.

Fiedrowicz, Michael. *Apologie im frühen Christentum: Die Kontroverse um den christlichen Wahrheitsanspruch in den ersten Jahrhunderten*, 3rd ed. Paderborn: Schöningh, 2005.

Fohrer, Georg. *Das Buch Hiob*, KAT. 2nd ed. Gütersloh: Gütersloher, 1988.

Forstmann, Jack. "Barth, Schleiermacher and The Christian Faith." *USQR* 21 (1966) 305–19.

Frame, John M. *Apologetics to the Glory of God: An Introduction*. Phillipsburg, NJ: P&R, 1994.

Frevel, Christian. "'Jetzt habe ich erkannt, dass YHWH größer ist als alle Götter.' Ex 18 und seine kompositionsgeschichtliche Stellung im Pentateuch." *BZ, NF* 47 (2003) 3–22.

Frydrych, Tomáš. *Living Under the Sun: Examination of Proverbs and Qoheleth.* VT.S 90. Leiden: Brill, 2002.

Geisler, Norman L. *Baker Encyclopedia of Christian Apologetics,* 9th ed. Grand Rapids: Baker, 2007.

Gertz, Jan Christian. "Antibabylonische Polemik im priesterlichen Schöpfungsbericht?" *ZThK* 106 (2009) 137–55.

———. "Babel im Rücken und das Land vor Augen: Anmerkungen zum Abschluss der Urgeschichte und zum Anfang der Erzählung von den Erzeltern Israels." In *Die Erzväter in der biblischen Tradition: Festschrift für Matthias Köckert,* edited by Anselm C. Hagedorn and Henrik Pfeiffer, 9–34. BZAW 400. Berlin: De Gruyter, 2009.

Giorgetti, Andrew. "The 'Mock Building Account' of Genesis 11:1–9: Polemic against Mesopotamian Royal Ideology." *VT* 64 (2014) 1–20. https://www.jstor.org/stable/43894095.

Gladd, Benjamin L. *Revealing the Mysterion: The Use of Mystery in Daniel and Second Temple Judaism with its Bearing on First Corinthians.* BZNW 160. Berlin: De Gruyter, 2008.

Goldingay, John E. *Daniel.* WBC. Dallas, TX: Word, 1989.

Gordis, Robert. "Religion, Wisdom and History in the Book of Esther—A New Solution to an Ancient Crux." *JBL* 100 (1981) 359–88. https://www.jstor.org/stable/3265960.

Graffy, Adrian. *A Prophet Confronts his People. The Disputation Speech in the Prophets,* AnBib 104. Rome: Biblical Institute Press, 1984.

Grisanti, Michael A. "The Missing Mandate: Missions in the Old Testament." In *Missions in a New Millennium: Change and Challenges in World Missions,* edited by W. Edward Glenny und William H. Smallman, 43–68. Grand Rapids: Kregel, 2000.

Grube, George Maximilan Anthony. "Apology." In *Plato. Complete Works,* edited by John M. Cooper, 17–36. Indianapolis, IN: Hackett, 1997.

Guerra, Anthony J. "Romans 4 as Apologetic Theology." *HThR* 81 (1988) 251–70. https://www.jstor.org/stable/1509704.

———. *Romans and the Apologetic Tradition: The Purpose, Genre and Audience of Paul's Letter.* SNTS.MS 81. Cambridge: University Press, 1995.

Gunkel, Hermann. "Einleitungen." Introduction to Hans Schmidt, *Die großen Propheten,* ix–lxx. SAT, 2nd ed. Göttingen: Vandenhoeck & Ruprecht 1923.

———. *Creation and Chaos in the Primeval Era and the Eschaton: A Religio-Historical Study of Genesis 1 and Revelation 12.* Translated by K. William Whitney. Grand Rapids: Eerdmans, 2006.

———. *Schöpfung und Chaos in Urzeit und Endzeit: Eine religionsgeschichtliche Untersuchung über Gen 1 und Ap Joh 12.* Göttingen: Vandenhoeck & Ruprecht, 1895.

Gupta, Nijay K. "'They Are Not Gods!' Jewish and Christian Idol Polemic and Greco-Roman Use of Cult Statues." *CBQ* 76 (2014) 704–19.

Hasel, Gerhard F. *Old Testament Theology. Basic Issues in the Current Debate*, 4th ed. Grand Rapids: Eerdmans, 1991.

———. "The Polemic Nature of the Genesis Cosmology." *EQ* 46 (1974) 81–102. https://biblicalstudies.org.uk/pdf/eq/1974-2_081.pdf.

———. "The Significance of the Cosmology in Gen 1 in Relation to Ancient Near Eastern Parallels." *AUSS* 10 (1972) 1–20. https://digitalcommons.andrews.edu/cgi/viewcontent.cgi?article=1216&context=auss.

Hatch, Edwin and Redpath, Henry A. *A Concordance to the Septuagint and the Other Greek Versions of the Old Testament (Including the Apocryphal Books), Vol. 1.* Grand Rapids: Baker, 1897. https://archive.org/details/HatchRedpath1.

Heffern, Andrew D. *Apology and Polemic in the New Testament.* New York: MacMillan, 1922.

Hermisson, Hans-Jürgen. "Diskussionsworte bei Deuterojesaja." *EvTh* 31 (1971) 665–80.

———. "Weisheit." In *Altes Testament*, 5th ed., edited by Hans Jochen Boecker et al., 200–25. Neukirchen-Vluyn: Neukirchener, 1996.

Hettema, Theo L. and van der Kooij, Arie, eds. *Religious Polemics in Context.* Papers presented to the Second International Conference of the Leiden Institute for the Study of Religions (LISOR) held at Leiden, April 27–28, 2000, STAR 11. Assen: Van Gorcum, 2004.

Hettema, Theo L. "The Noble Art of Self-Defence: Schleiermacher and Von Clausewitz on Theological Polemics and the Theory of Warfare." In *Religious Polemics in Context*, edited by Theo L. Hettema and Arie van der Kooij, 21–31. STAR 11. Assen: Van Gorcum, 2004.

Hilbrands, Walter. "Zehn Thesen zum biblischen Schöpfungsbericht (Gen 1,1–2,3) aus exegetischer Sicht," *JETh* 18, edited by Rolf Hille et al., 7–25. Wuppertal: Brockhaus, 2004. https://www.afet.de/download/2004/Hilbrands2004.pdf.

———. "Die Länge der Schöpfungstage. Eine exegetische und rezeptionsgeschichtliche Untersuchung von יוֹם ('Tag') in Gen 1,1–2,3." *BN* 149 (2011) 3–12.

Hinson, Ed. "Apologetics, Biblical." In *The Popular Encyclopedia of Apologetics. Surveying the Evidence for the Truth of Christianity*, edited by Ed Hinson and Ergun Cancer, 28–31. Eugene, OR: Harvest House, 2008.

Holladay, William L. *Jeremiah 2: A Commentary on the Book of the Prophet Jeremiah Chapters 26–52.* Hermeneia. Minneapolis: Fortress, 1989.

Holter, Knut. *Second Isaiah's Idol Fabrication Passages.* BET 28. Frankfurt am Main: Lang, 1995.

Houtman, Cornelis. *Exodus, Volume 1.* Kampen: Kok 1993.

Janowski, Bernd. *Sühne als Heilsgeschehen. Traditions- und religionsgeschichtliche Studien zur Sühnetheologie der Priesterschrift*, 2nd ed. WMANT 55. Neukirchen-Vluyn: Neukirchener, 2000.

Jefford, Clayton N., ed. *The Epistle to Diognetus (With the Fragment of Quadratus). Introduction, Text, and Commentary.* Oxford: University Press, 2013.

Jelke, Robert. "Die Aufgabe der Dogmatik." *NKZ* 40 (1929) 42.

Jongeneel, Jan A. B. *Philosophy, Science and Theology of Mission in the 19th and 20th Centuries: A Missiological Encyclopedia, Part I: The Philosophy and Science of Mission.* SIHC 92. Frankfurt am Main: Lang, 1995.

Jonker, Louis C. "Religious Polemics in Exile: The Creator God of Genesis 1." In *Religious Polemics in Context,* edited by Theo L. Hettema and Arie van der Kooij, 235–54. STAR 11. Assen: Van Gorcum, 2004.

Kamlah, Erhard. "Apologetik I. Apologetik und Polemik im NT." In *RGG*³ 1 (1957) 477–80.

Kapelrud, Arvid S. "The Mythological Features in Genesis Chapter I and the Author's Intentions." *VT* 24 (1974) 178–96. https://www.jstor.org/stable/1517124.

Kellermann, Ulrich. "*apologeomai* sich verteidigen *apologia* Verteidigungsrede." *EWNT* 1 (1980, ³2011) 329–30.

Keown, Gerald L., et al. *Jeremiah 26–52.* WBC. Waco, TX: Word, 1995.

Knorre, Peter von. *Vergeblicher Gottesdienst: Die kultpolemischen Texte im Alten Testament.* SBB 65. Stuttgart: Katholisches Bibelwerk, 2010.

Koch, Klaus. *Amos: Untersucht mit den Mitteln strukturaler Formgeschichte.* Bd. 1. AOAT 30. Kevelaer: Butzon & Bercker, 1976.

Koorevaar, Hendrik J. "Exodus—Levitikus—Numeri: Durchdringen ins heilige Herz der Tora." In *Themenbuch zur Theologie des Alten Testaments,* edited by Herbert H. Klement and Julius Steinberg, 87–131. Wuppertal: Brockhaus, 2007.

———. "Psalm 82: Wie zijn de Goden?" In *Moeilijke Psalmen,* edited by A.G. Knevel, 57–69. Kampen: Kok Voorhoeve, 1992.

———. "The Books of Exodus, Leviticus and Numbers, and the Macro-Structural Problem of the Pentateuch." In *The Books of Leviticus and Numbers,* edited by Thomas Römer, 423–53. BETL 215. Leuven: Peeters, 2008.

———. "The Exile and Return Model: A Proposal for the Original Macrostructure of the Hebrew Canon." *JETS* 57 (2014) 501–12. https://www.etsjets.org/files/JETS-PDFs/57/57-3/JETS_57-3_501-12_Koorevaar.pdf.

———. "The Torah as One, Three or Five Books: An Introduction to the Macro-Structural Problem of the Pentateuch." *Hiphil* 3 (2006) 1–19. http://see-j.net/index.php/hiphil/article/view/28/25.

———. "The Torah Model as Original Macrostructure of the Hebrew Canon: a Critical Evaluation." *ZAW* 122 (2010) 64–80.

Koorevaar, Hendrik J. and Paul, Mart-Jan, eds. *Theologie van het Oude Testament: De blijvende boodschap van de Hebreeuwse Bijbel.* Zoetermeer: Boekencentrum, 2013.

Kraus, Hans-Joachim. *Prophetie in der Krisis. Studien zu Texten aus dem Buch Jeremia*. BSt 43. Neukirchen-Vluyn: Neukirchener, 1964.
Kustermann, Abraham Peter. *Die Apologetik Johann Sebastian Dreys. Kritische, historische und systematische Untersuchung zu Forschungsgeschichte, Programmentwicklung, Status und Gehalt*. Tübingen: Mohr/Siebeck, 1988.
Lampe, Peter and Samley, J. Paul, eds. *Paul and Rhetoric*. New York: Continuum, 2010.
Lanczkowski, Günter. *Begegnung und Wandel der Religionen*. Düsseldorf: Diederichs, 1971.
Leiman, Sid Z. *The Canonization of Hebrew Scripture. The Talmudic and Midrashic Evidence*. Hamden, CT: Archon, 1976.
Leiner, Martin. *Methodischer Leitfaden Systematische Theologie und Religionsphilosophie*. Göttingen: Vandenhoeck & Ruprecht, 2008.
Lemme, Ludwig. "Apologetik, Apologie." RE^3 1 (1896) 679–98.
Lenzi, Alan. "Secrecy, Textual Legitimation, and Intercultural Polemics in the Book of Daniel." *CBQ* 71 (2009) 330–48. https://www.jstor.org/stable/43726545.
Levinson, P. Navè. "Apologetik 1. Jüdisch." In *Lexikon religiöser Grundbegriffe. Judentum Christentum Islam*, 2nd ed., edited by Adel Theodor Khoury, 47–50. Wiesbaden: Marix, 2007.
Lewis, Clive Staples. *God in the Dock*. Grand Rapids: Eerdmans, 1970.
Liddell, Henry George, Scott, Robert and Jones, Henry Stuart. *A Greek-English Lexicon*, 9th ed. London: Clarendon, 1948.
Liedke, Gerhard. "*rīb* streiten." *THAT* 2 (1975, ^{4}1993) 771–77.
Lim, Timothy H. *The Formation of the Jewish Canon*. AYBRL. New Haven, CT: Yale University Press, 2013.
Lindars, Barnabas. *New Testament Apologetic: The Doctrinal Significance of the Old Testament Quotations*. London: SCM, 1961.
Louw, Johannes P. and Nida, Eugene A. *Greek-English Lexicon of the New Testament Based on Semantic Domains, vol. 1: Introduction & Domains*. New York: United Bible Societies, 1998.
Lucas, Ernest C. "Wisdom Theology." *DOTW* (2008) 901–12.
Lüdemann, Gerd. "Apologetik III. Neues Testament." In RGG^4 1 (1998) 614–16.
MacIntyre, Alisdair. *After Virtue: A Study in Moral Theory*. Notre Dame, IN: Notre Dame University Press, 1981.
Martin-Archard, Robert. *A Light to the Nations: A Study of the Old Testament's Conception of Israel's Mission to the World*. Edinburgh: Oliver and Boyd, 1962.
Mascord, Keith A. *Alvin Plantinga and Christian Apologetic*. Paternoster Theological Monographs. Milton Keynes, UK: Paternoster, 2006.
McCann, J. Clinton. "The Single Most Important Text in the Entire Bible. Toward a Theology of the Psalms." In *Soundings in the Theology of Psalms. Perspectives and Methods in Contemporary Scholarship*, edited by Rolf A. Jacobson, 63–75. Minneapolis: Fortress, 2011.

McGrath, Alister E. *Mere Apologetics: How to Help Seekers and Skeptics Find Faith*. Grand Rapids: Baker, 2012.

———. "Evangelical Apologetics." *BS* 155 (1998) 3–10. https://theologicalstudies.org.uk/article_apol_mcgrath.html.

Morley, Brian K. *Mapping Apologetics. Comparing Contemporary Approaches*. Downers Grove, IL: InterVarsity Press Academic, 2015.

Neagoe, Alexandru. *The Trial of the Gospel. An Apologetic Reading of Luke's Trial Narratives*. SNTS.MS 116. Cambridge: University Press, 2008.

Nestle, Wilhelm. "Zur altchristlichen Apologetik im Neuen Testament." *ZRG* 4 (1952) 115–23.

Nowak, Kurt. *Schleiermacher. Leben, Werk und Wirkung*. Göttingen: Vandenhoeck & Ruprecht, 2001.

Okoye, James Chukwuma. *Israel and the Nations. A Mission Theology of the Old Testament*. Maryknoll, NY: Orbis, 2006.

Omerzu, Heike. "Apologetics III. New Testament." *EBR* 2 (2009) 426–31.

Ott, Heinrich. *Apologetik des Glaubens: Grundprobleme einer dialogischen Fundamentaltheologie*. Darmstadt: Wissenschaftliche Buchgesellschaft, 1994.

Otto, Eckart. "Brückenschläge in der Pentateuchforschung." *ThR* 64 (1999) 84–99.

Petry, Sven. *Die Entgrenzung JHWHs*. FAT 2/27. Tübingen: Mohr/Siebeck, 2007.

Planck, Gottlieb Jakob. *Einleitung in die Theologischen Wissenschaften*. Theil 1. Leipzig: Crusius, 1794. https://books.google.de/books?id=Nj1hAAAAcAAJ.

Plantinga, Alvin. "Self-Profile." In *Alvin Plantinga*, edited by James E. Tomberlin and Peter van Inwagen, 3–97. Dordrecht: Reidel, 2012.

Powell, Doug. *Holman QuickSource Guide to Christian Apologetics*. Nashville: Holman, 2006.

Preuß, Horst Dietrich. *Theologie des Alten Testaments. Band 1: JHWHs erwählendes und verpflichtendes Handeln*. Stuttgart: Kohlhammer, 1991.

———. *Verspottung fremder Religionen im Alten Testament*. BWANT 92. Stuttgart: Kohlhammer, 1971.

Propp, William Henry C. *Exodus 1–18: A New Translation with Introduction and Commentary*. AB. New York: Doubleday, 1999.

Provan, Iain. *Seriously Dangerous Religion: What the Old Testament Really Says and Why it Matters*. Waco, TX: Baylor University Press, 2014.

Rad, Gerhard von. *Genesis: A Commentary*, 2nd ed. Translated by John H. Marks. OTL. Philadelphia: Westminster, 1972.

———. *Das erste Buch Mose: Genesis*, 9th ed. ATD 2/4. Göttingen: Vandenhoeck & Ruprecht, 1972.

———. *Old Testament Theology, Volume I: The Theology of Israel's Historical Traditions*, 2nd ed. Translated by D. M. G. Stalker. OTL. Louisville: Westminster, 2001.

BIBLIOGRAPHY

———. *Theologie des Alten Testaments: Band I. Die Theologie der geschichtlichen Überlieferung Israels*, 10th ed. München: Kaiser, 1992.
———. *Weisheit in Israel*, 3rd ed. Neukirchen-Vluyn: Neukirchener, 1985
———. *Wisdom in Israel*. Translated by James D. Martin. Harrisburg, PN: Trinity, 1972.
Ramm, Bernard L. *Protestant Christian Evidences: A Textbook of the Evidences of the Truthfulness of the Christian Faith for Conservative Protestants*. Chicago: Moody, 1953.
———. "The Apologetic of the Old Testament. The Basis of a Biblical and Christian Apologetic." *BETS* 1 (1958) 15–20. https://biblicalstudies.org.uk/pdf/bets/vol01/apologetic_ramm.pdf.
———. *The God Who Makes a Difference: A Christian Appeal to Reason*. Waco, TX: Word, 1972.
Reid, Garnett. "'Thus You Will Say to Them': A Cross-Cultural Confessional Polemic in Jeremiah 10.11." *JSOT* 31 (2006) 221–38.
Reid, J.K.S. "Apologetic Elements in the New Testament." In his book, *Christian Apologetics*, 15–35. Grand Rapids: Eerdmans, 1969.
Rendtorff, Rolf. "Die Hermeneutik einer kanonischen Theologie des Alten Testaments. Prolegomena." In *Religionsgeschichte Israels oder Theologie des Alten Testaments?*, edited by Bernd Janowski and Norbert Lohfink, 35–44. JBTh 10. Neukirchen-Vluyn: Neukirchener, 1995.
———. *Theologie des Alten Testaments. Ein Kanonischer Entwurf. Band 1. Kanonische Grundlegung*. Neukirchen-Vluyn: Neukirchener, 1999.
Reymond, Robert L. *The Justification of Knowledge: An Introductory Study in Christian Apologetic Methodology*. Philippsburg, NJ: Presbyterian & Reformed, 1976.
Richardson, Alan. *Christian Apologetics*, 8th ed. London: SCM, 1970.
Riecker, Siegbert. "Alttestamentliche Grundlagen der Apologetik. Ein biblisch-theologischer Entwurf." *ZKTh* 138 (2016) 1–27.
———. *Ein Priestervolk für alle Völker: Der Segensauftrag Israels für alle Nationen in der Tora und den Vorderen Propheten*. SBB 59. Stuttgart: Katholisches Bibelwerk, 2007.
———. "Exegetische Begründung des apologetischen Auftrags." In *Verantwortlich glauben: Ein Themenbuch zur christlichen Apologetik*, edited by Christian Herrmann and Rolf Hille, 23–37. Nürnberg: VTR, 2016.
———. *Mission im Alten Testament? Ein Forschungsüberblick mit Auswertung*. Beiheft Interkulturelle Theologie 10. Frankfurt am Main: Lembeck, 2008.
———. "Missions in the Hebrew Bible Revisited: Four Theological Trails Instead of One Confining Concept." *Missiology* 44 (2016) 324–39.
Römer, Thomas. "La création des hommes et leur multiplication: Lecture comparée d'Athra-Hasis, de Gilgamesh XI et de Genèse 1." *Sem.* 55 (2013) 147–56.

Rose, Martin. *Der Ausschließlichkeitsanspruch Jahwes: Deuteronomistische Schultheologie und die Volksfrömmigkeit in der späten Königszeit*. BWANT 106. Stuttgart: Kohlhammer, 1975.

Rössler, Martin. *Schleiermachers Programm der philosophischen Theologie*. Berlin: De Gruyter, 1994.

Roth, Wolfgang M. W. "For Life, he Appeals to Death (Wis 13:18). A Study of Old Testament Idol Parodies." *CBQ* 37 (1975) 21–47. https://www.jstor.org/stable/43715267.

Ruppert, Lothar. *Die Josephserzählung der Genesis: Ein Beitrag zur Theologie der Pentateuchquellen*. StANT 11. München: Kösel, 1965.

———. *Genesis: Ein kritischer und theologischer Kommentar, Tlbd. 1, Gen 1,1–11,26*. FzB 70. Würzburg: Echter, 1992.

———. "'Urgeschichte' oder Urgeschehen? Zur Interpretation von Gen. 1–11." *MThZ* 30 (1979) 19–32.

Sack, Karl Heinrich. *Christliche Apologetik*, 2nd ed. Hamburg: Perthes, 1841. https://archive.org/details/christlicheapoloosackgoog.

Sager, Dirk. *Polyphonie des Elends. Psalm 9/10 im konzeptionellen Diskurs und literarischen Kontext*. FAT 2/21. Tübingen: Mohr/Siebeck, 2006.

Sailhamer, John. *The Pentateuch as Narrative: A Biblical-Theological Commentary*. Grand Rapids: Zondervan, 1992.

Sarna, Nahum M. *Exploring Exodus: The Origins of Biblical Israel*. New York: Socken, 1986.

Scheurer, Erich. *Altes Testament und Mission: Zur Begründung des Missionsauftrages*, 2nd ed. Gießen: Brunnen, 1999.

Schleiermacher, Friedrich Daniel Ernst. *Brief Outline of Theology as a Field of Study: Revised Translation of the 1811 and 1830 Editions with Essays and Notes by Terrence N. Tice*, 3rd ed. Translated by Terrence N. Tice. Louisville: Westminster, 2011.

———. *Kurze Darstellung des theologischen Studiums zum Behulf einleitender Vorlesungen (1811/1830)*, edited by Dirk Schmid. Berlin: De Gruyter, 2002.

———. *The Christian Faith: With an Introduction by Paul T. Nimmo*, 3rd ed. Translated by Terrence N. Tice et al. London: T. & T. Clark, 2016.

———. *Theologische Enzyklopädie (1831/32): Nachschrift David Friedrich Strauss*, edited by Walter Sachs, Schleiermacher-Archiv 4. Berlin: De Gruyter, 1987.

Schmidt, Hans. *Die großen Propheten*. SAT. Göttingen: Vandenhoeck & Ruprecht, 1914, ²1923.

Schmid, Konrad. "Von der Gegenwelt zur Lebenswelt. Evolutionäre Kosmologie und Theologie im Buch Genesis." In *Cosmologies et cosmogonies dans la littérature antique: Huit exposés suivis d'une discussion et d'un épilogue*, edited by Michael Erler, Therese Fuhrer and Pascale Derron, 51–104. EnAC 61. Genève: Droz, 2015.

Schmidt, Werner H. *Alttestamentlicher Glaube*, 10th ed. Neukirchen-Vluyn: Neukirchener, 2007.

———. *The Faith of the Old Testament: A History*. Translated by John Sturdy. Philadelphia: Westminster, 1983.

Schreiner, Helmuth. *Geist und Gestalt. Vom Ringen um eine neue Verkündigung*, 2nd ed. Schwerin: Bahn, 1927.

Schüle, Andreas. *Der Prolog der hebräischen Bibel. Der literar - und theologiegeschichtliche Diskurs der Urgeschichte (Gen 1–11)*. ATANT 86. Zürich: TVZ 2006.

———. *Die Urgeschichte (Genesis 1–11)*. ZBK. Zürich: TVZ, 2009.

Schultz, Richard. "'Und sie verkünden meine Herrlichkeit unter den Nationen.' Mission im Alten Testament unter besonderer Berücksichtigung von Jesaja." In *Werdet meine Zeugen. Weltmission im Horizont von Theologie und Geschichte*, edited by Hans Kasdorf and Friedemann Walldorf, 33–53. Neuhausen-Stuttgart: Hänssler, 1996.

Scott, Ernest Findlay. *The Apologetic of the New Testament*. London: Willams & Norgate, 1907. https://archive.org/details/apologeticofnewtooscotuoft.

Searle, John R. "A Classification of Illocutionary Acts." *Lang. Soc.* 5 (1976) 1–23. https://www.jstor.org/stable/4166848.

———. *Expression and Meaning. Studies in the Theory of Speech Acts*. Cambridge: University Press, 1979.

Seckler, Max. "Apologetik I. Begriff." In *LThK*^{3} 1 (1993) 834–36.

———. "Apologetik II. Biblisch." In *LThK*^{3} 1 (1993) 836–37.

———. "Apologetik IV. Systematisch." In *LThK*^{3} 1 (1993) 839–42.

Seebass, Horst. *Genesis I. Urgeschichte (1,1–11,26)*. Neukirchen-Vluyn: Neukirchener, 1996.

———. *Numeri, Teilband 2: Kapitel 10,11–21,1*. BKAT. Neukirchen-Vluyn: Neukirchener, 2003.

Seow, Choon Leong. "From Mountain to Mountain. The Reign of God in Daniel 2." In *A God So Near: Essays on Old Testament Theology in Honor of Patrick D. Miller*, edited by Brent A. Straw and Nancy R. Bowen, 355–74. Winona Lake, IN: Eisenbrauns, 2003.

Sire, James W. *A Little Primer on Humble Apologetics*. Downers Grove, IL: InterVarsity, 2006.

Skarsaune, Oskar. "Apologie II. Schrifttum," In *RGG*^{4} 1 (1998) 631–32.

Smith, Mark S. "The Polemic of Biblical Monotheism: Outsider Context and Insider Referentiality in Second Isaiah." In *Religious Polemics in Context*, edited by Theo L. Hettema and Arie van der Kooij, 201–34. STAR 11. Assen: Van Gorcum, 2004.

Snoek, Jan A. M. "Religious Polemics in Context: An Annotated Bibliography." In *Religious Polemics in Context*, edited by Theo L. Hettema and Arie van der Kooij, 507–88. STAR 11. Assen: Van Gorcum, 2004.

Stackhouse, John Gordon. *Humble Apologetics: Defending the Faith Today*. Oxford: University Press, 2002.

Stanton, Graham N. "Aspects of Early Christian-Jewish Polemic and Apologetic." *NTS* 31 (1985) 377–92.

Steck, Karl Gerhard. "Apologetik II. Neuzeit." In *TRE* 3 (1978) 411–24.

BIBLIOGRAPHY

Steinberg, Julius. *Die Ketuvim. Ihr Aufbau und ihre Botschaft.* BBB 152. Hamburg: Philo, 2006.

———. "Gottes Ordnungen verstehen und leben. Eine Theologie der alttestamentlichen Weisheit." In *Freude an Gottes Weisung. Themenbuch zur Theologie des Alten Testaments*, 2nd ed., edited by Herbert H. Klement and Julius Steinberg, 211–37. Riehen: arteMedia, 2012.

Stenschke, Christoph. "Apologetik, Polemik und Mission: Der Umgang mit der Religiosität der 'anderen.'" In *Weltauffassung – Kult – Ethos*, edited by Jürgen Zangenberg, 244–53. Neues Testament und Antike Kultur 3. Neukirchen-Vluyn: Neukirchener, 2011.

Thiselton, Anthony C. *New Horizons in Hermeneutics: The Theory and Pracitce of Transforming Biblical Reading.* Grand Rapids: Zondervan, 1992.

Tillich, Paul. *Systematic Theology, Volume 1.* Chicago: University of Chicago Press, 1951.

Trotter, James M. "Death of the אלהים in Psalm 82." *JBL* 131 (2012) 221–39. https://www.jstor.org/stable/23488222.

Tsumura, David Toshio. *The Earth and the Waters in Genesis 1 and 2: A Linguistic Investigation.* JSOT.S 83. Sheffield: JSOT Press, 1989.

Uehlinger, Christoph. "Medien altorientalischer Theologien: Antwort an Karel van der Toorn." In *Theologie in Israel und in den Nachbarkulturen: Beiträge des Symposiums „Das Alte Testament und die Kultur der Moderne" anlässlich des 100. Geburtstags Gerhard von Rads (1901–1971), Heidelberg, 18.–21. Oktober 2001*, edited by Manfred Oeming et al., 125–78. ATM 9. Münster: Lit, 2004.

———. *Weltreich und "eine Rede". Eine neue Deutung der sogenannten Turmbauerzählung (Gen 11,1–9).* OBO 101. Göttingen: Vandenhoeck & Ruprecht, 1990.

Usarski, Frank. "Apologetik I. Zum Begriff." In *RGG*[4] 1 (1998) 661.

Verweyen, Hansjürgen. *Einführung in die Fundamentaltheologie.* Darmstadt: Wissenschaftliche Buchgesellschaft, 2008.

Vos, Johan S. *Die Kunst der Argumentation bei Paulus.* WUNT 149. Tübingen: Mohr/Siebeck, 2002.

Wagner, Harald. "Apologetik V. In der prot. Theologie." In *LThK*[3] 1 (1993) 842–44.

Warfield, Benjamin B. "Apologetics." In *The New Schaff-Herzog Encyclopedia of Religious Knowledge, Volume I*, edited by Samuel MacAuley Jackson, 232–88. New York: Funk and Wagnalis, 1908. Reprint, *Studies in Theology*, 3–21. The Works of Benjamin B. Warfield 9. Rev. ed. Grand Rapids: Baker, 1981.

Weber, Beat. *Werkbuch Psalmen II: Die Psalmen 73 bis 150.* Stuttgart: Kohlhammer, 2003.

Wenham, Gordon J. *Exploring the Old Testament, Volume I: The Pentateuch.* London: SPCK, 2003.

———. *Numbers.* TOTC. Leicester: InterVarsity, 1981.

Wernle, Paul. "Altchristliche Apologetik im Neuen Testament." *ZNW* 1 (1900) 42–65.
Westermann, Claus. "Sprache und Struktur der Prophetie Deuterojesajas." In *Forschung am Alten Testament. Gesammelte Studien*, edited by Claus Westermann, 92–170. München: Kaiser, 1964. Reprint, *Sprache und Struktur der Prophetie Deuterojesajas, mit einer Literaturübersicht "Hauptlinien der Deuterojesaja-Forschung von 1964–1979,"* edited by Claus Westermann and Andreas Richter. CThM 11. Stuttgart: Calwer, 1981.
Westermann, Claus. *Genesis, Vol. I: Genesis 1–11*, 4th ed. BKAT I/1. Neukirchen-Vluyn: Neukirchener, 1999.
———. *Grundformen Prophetischer Rede*, 5th ed. München: Kaiser, 1978.
———. *Lob und Klage in den Psalmen*, 6th ed. Göttingen: Vandenhoeck & Ruprecht, 1983.
Whybray, Roger Norman. *Proverbs*. NCB. London: Marshall Pickering, 1994.
———. *The Intellectual Tradition in the Old Testament*. BZAW 135. Berlin: De Gruyter, 1974.
Winter, Bruce W. "Official Proceedings and the Forensic Speeches in Acts 24–26." In *The Book of Acts in Its Ancient Literary Setting*, edited by Bruce W. Winter and Andrew D. Clarke, 305–36. BAFCS 1. Grand Rapids: Eerdmans, 1993.
Wolff, Hans Walter. *Das Zitat im Prophetenspruch. Eine Studie zur prophetischen Verkündigungsweise*. BhEvTh 4. München: Kaiser, 1937. Reprint, *Gesammelte Studien*, edited by Hans Walter Wolff, 36–129. München: Kaiser, 1964.
———. *Prophetische Alternativen. Entdeckungen des Neuen im Alten Testament*. München: Kaiser, 1982.
Zöckler, Otto. *Geschichte der Apologie des Christentums*. Gütersloh: Bertelsmann, 1907.

Author Index

Adam, Alfred, 4–5, 13, 15–19
Aland, Kurt, 2, 15, 19
Albertz, Rainer, 23
Alexander, T. Desmond, 28
Amit, Yairah, 21, 25
Ammann, Sonja, 49
Antiphon of Rhamnus, 1
Apollinaris Claudius, 3
Aristides of Athens, 3
Aristotle, 1
Athenagoras of Athens, 3
Austin, John L., 90

Bahnsen, Greg L., 20
Barker, William D., 49
Barnard, Leslie Willam, 1
Barth, Karl, 5, 9–15
Bauks, Michaela, 32
Bayer, Oswald, 4
Beattie, Francis R., 5
Becking, Bob, 46
Beilby, James K., 4, 6, 18
Beißer, Friedrich, 16, 18–19
Berger, Klaus, 20–21
Berkouwer, Gerrit Cornelis, 4
Berlejung, Angelika, 51
Birkner, Hans-Joachim, 7
Blenkinsopp, Joseph, 31
Blum, Erhard, 31
Boa, Kenneth D., 5, 20
Bowman, Robert M., 5, 20

Bruce, Frederick Fyvie, xiii, 50
Brueggemann, Walter, 44
Brunner, Emil, 4, 11–12, 17
Bührer, Walter, 31

Carnell, Edward J., 6
Carr, David, 36
Chazan, Robert, xiv, 6, 38, 44
Chisholm, Robert B., 43
Clemens of Alexandria, 3
Clements, Ronald E., 88
Clifford, Richard J., 51
Coats, George W., 31
Cooper, John M., 1
Cowan, Steven B., 4
Crenshaw, James L., 74, 83, 85
Crossan, John D., 58

Dascal, Marcelo, 21
Dick, Michael Brennan, 51
Dillmann, August, 40
Diogenetus, xv
Dohmen, Christoph, 51
Donald Evans, 91
Drey, Johann Sebastian von, 7, 19–20
Droge, Arthur J., xiii
Dulles, Avery, xiii, 7
Dumbrell, William J., 37
Dyrness, William A., 4, 30

Author Index

Emanuel, David, 53
Enger, Peter A., 41
Eusebius of Caesarea, 3

Ferguson, Everett, xv
Fiedrowicz, Michael, 1, 3
Fohrer, Georg, 68
Forstmann, Jack, 9
Frame, John, 5
Frevel, Christian, 41
Frydrych, Tomáš, 69

Geisler, Norman L., 4
Gertz, Jan Christian, 33–34, 37
Giorgetti, Andrew, 37
Gladd, Benjamin L., 63
Goldingay, John E., 63
Gordis, Roberg, 60
Graffy, Adrian, 70–72
Grisanti, Michael A., vii
Grube, George M.A., 1
Guerra, Anthony J., 20
Gunkel, Hermann, 32, 34, 70
Gupta, Nijay K., 51

Hasel, Gerhard F., 24, 32, 88
Hatch, Edwin, 3
Heffern, Andrew D., xiii
Hepp, Valentin, 4
Hermisson, Hans-Jürgen, 69, 71
Hettema, Theo L., 21
Hilbrands, Walter, 31, 32
Hinson, Ed, xiv
Holladay, William L., 45
Holter, Knut, 51
Houtman, Cornelis, 39, 41

Janowski, Bernd, 31
Jefford, Clayton N., xv
Jelke, Robert, 13
Jones, Henry Stuart, 1
Jongeneel, Jan A. B., xiii
Jonker, Louis C., 31
Justin Martyr, 3

Kamlah, Erhard, xiii
Kapelrud, Arvid S., 32
Kellermann, Ulrich, 2
Keown, Gerald L., 77
Knorre, Peter von, 22
Koch, Klaus, 71
Koorevaar, Hendrik J., 24, 28, 39, 58
Kraus, Hans-Joachim, 56, 77
Kustermann, Abraham Peter, 7

Lampe, Peter, xiii
Lanczkowski, Günther, 22
Leiner, Martin, 17
Lemme, Ludwig, 13
Lenzi, Alan, 62
Levinson, P. Navè, xiv, 62
Lewis, Clive Staples, 6
Liddell, Henry George, 1
Liedke, Gerhard, 3
Lindars, Barnabas, xv
Louw, Johannes P., 3
Lucas, Ernest C., 69
Lüdemann, Gerd, xiii

MacIntyre, Alisdair, 46
Maran, Prudent, 3
Martin-Archard, Robert, 62
Mascord, Keith A., 4
McCann, J. Clinton, 58
McGrath, Alister, 6
Melito of Sardes, 3
Miltiades, 3
Minucius Felix, 3
Morel, Frédéric, 3
Morley, Brian K., xiv

Neagoe, Alexandru, 20
Nestle, Wilhelm, xiii
Nida, Eugene A., 3
Nowak, Kurt, 9

Okoye, James Chukwuma, xiii
Omerzu, Heike, xiii
Ott, Heinrich, 5, 14

Author Index

Otto, Eckart, 37

Pascal, Blaise, 17
Paul, Mart-Jan, 24
Petry, Sven, 51
Planck, Gottlieb Jakob, 8
Plantinga, Alvin, 4
Plato, 1
Powell, Doug, 6
Preuß, Horst Dietrich, 24, 26, 31, 33, 38, 43, 58, 60, 62, 86, 88
Propp, William H.C., 38, 41

Quadratus, 3

Rad, Gerhard von, 24, 31, 33, 49, 88
Ramm, Bernard L., 5-6, 25, 50, 62, 83
Redpath, Henry A., 3
Reid, Garnett, 50
Reid, J.K.S., xiii
Rendtorff, Rolf, 24
Reymond, Robert L., 5
Richard Biggs, 91
Richardson, Alan, 5, 20
Riecker, Siegbert, vii-viii, xiii, 41, 62
Römer, Thomas, 33
Rose, Martin, 22
Roth, Wolfgang M.W., 51
Ruppert, Lothar, 31, 38

Sack, Karl Heinrich, 7, 19-20
Sager, Dirk, 66
Sailhamer, John, 28
Samley, J. Paul, xiii
Sarna, Nahum M., 38
Scalise, Pamela J., 77
Scheurer, Erich, xiii, 58
Schleiermacher, Friedrich, 7-18, 21
Schmid, Konrad, 34
Schmidt, Werner H., 32, 48
Schreiner, Helmuth, 4
Schüle, Andreas, 33-34, 37
Schultz, Richard, 22
Scott, Ernest Findlay, xiii

Scott, Robert, 1
Searle, John R., 90-91
Seckler, Max, xiv, 4, 14, 16
Seebass, Horst, 37, 40
Seow, Choon L., 63
Sire, James W., 5
Skarsaune, Oskar, 3
Smith, Mark S., 48, 51
Smothers, Thomas G., 77
Snoek, Jan A.M., 22
Socrates, 1
Stackhouse, John Gordon, 4
Stanton, Graham N., xiii
Steck, Karl Gerhard, 8, 11, 18
Steinberg, Julius, 27, 60, 69
Stenschke, Christoph, xiii

Tatian, 3
Tertullian, 3
Theophilus of Anitochia, 3
Thiselton, Anthony C., 90-91
Thucydides, 1
Tillich, Paul, 4
Trotter, James M., 58
Tsumura, David Toshio, 32

Uehlinger, Christoph, 37, 88
Usarski, Frank, 5

Verweyen, Hansjürgen, 14
Vos, Johan S., xiii

Wagner, Harald, 14
Warfield, Benjamin B., 7
Weber, Beat, 53
Wenham, Gordon J., 28, 39
Wernle, Paul, xiii
Westermann, Claus, 37, 70-71, 83, 88
Whybray, Roger N., 69
Winter, Bruce W., 21
Wolff, Hans Walter, 56, 70, 83

Zimmerli, Walther, 88
Zöckler, Otto, 16, 19

Subject Index

absoluteness claim, 16
accusation, 1–3, 20, 65, 68, 81–83, 89
ad absurdum, 73
adultery, 68
advice, 66
Ahab, 80
Ahaz, 79
ambivalence, 85
Ammon, 44, 57, 86, 87
Amun/Amon, 38, 57
animals, 54
another task, 12
antimythical, 31
antithetische Verkündigung, 70–85
apologists, early Christian, 3
apology – apologetics, 7, 19–21
Apology of Socrates, 1
apostasy, 23, 82
Aram, 44
Aramaic, 50
ark of the covenant, 43
arrogance, 80, 81
art of defense, 16, 18
Assyria, 44, 87
astral deities, 31, 33, 38, 48
atheism, 64, 68
Atraḫasis epic, 36
attack, 4, 18, 21, 51

authority, 10, 27, 36, 53, 82, 85, 87

Baʿal, 38, 43, 49, 86
Baba Bathra 14b, 27
Babylon, 34, 44, 50, 54, 58, 76–77, 87
Bel, 53, 58
bənê ʿelyôn, 58
benefit, 68–69, 84
Bestreitung, 70
biblical theology, 17, 19–29
blessing, 37, 65
blindness, 64, 68, 79
Book of Wisdom, 60
bride, 83
building reports, 31
burden of Yhwh, 82

Canaan, 41, 42–43, 74, 86
canonical approach, 23–24, 26–29
Carmel, 86
carrying, 54
Catholic church, 5, 7, 10, 14–15, 18
Chaldea, 44
Chemosh, 57
chiasm, 53
child, 38, 54, 58, 81, 84, 91
church authority, 10
citatory apologetics, 70–85

111

Subject Index

classification, 8, 28–29, 72, 91
comissive, 91
communication, 3, 50, 79, 86
community of faith, 6, 8–10, 16–17, 21
compassion, 74
confession, 61
confidence, 75, 76
conquest, 74, 86
conscience, 2, 75
construction report, 31
conversion, 62
counterwriting, 36
court, 1–3, 20, 71
covenant, 41, 75, 83–84
creation account, 29–35
creation narratives, 36
creator, 32, 48, 50
cult polemic, 22
curse, 65, 74
cynicism, 66

Dagon, 42
dead idols, 17, 25, 52
death, 43
deception, 72
defense, 5, 9
defense speech, 1–3, 20, 87
demons, 47
denouncement, 80–81
despair, 65
didactic, 31
didactics, 87
dietary rules, 87
directives, 90
disenchantment of nature, 34
Diskussionswort, 71
disobedience, 44
disputation, 70–85
disputation dialogue, 71
Disputationswort, 70
dispute, 62
diversity, 25, 88–89
diviner, 39

dogma, 11, 13
dogmatics, 12–13, 15, 18
doxology, 61

Egypt, 39, 37–42, 44–45, 57, 73, 87
election, 77, 79
ʾĕlōhîm, 47, 58
Epistle of Jeremiah, 51
Epistle to Diogenetus, xv, 3
eristics, 11
ethics, 46, 63, 68, 75, 82
etymology, 1–3, 18
exclusivism, 41, 43, 87
exemplary apologetics, 86–87
exile, 44, 62, 77
Exile and Return Model, 27
existence of God, 30, 63–65, 68
exodus, 37–42

faith, 11–12, 24, 63, 68, 81, 83, 87, 90
faithlessness, 68
false prophets, 23, 76, 78, 82, 86–87
fatalism, 64
fear of God, 68–69, 83
fiery furnace, 62
flood, 36
food, 32
fool, 68, 80
foreign religion, 22, 26
frog, 38
fulfillment, 55–56, 69, 74, 83–84, 89
fundamental theology, 14

golden calf, 73
Goliath, 86–87
goodness, 65
graduated view, 17
grape, 84

hammer and nails, 54
Hananiah, 77–78, 83, 86
Hapi, 38
heart, 2, 41, 87

Subject Index

hebel, 47, 54
Ḥeqet/Ḥeqtit, 38
hermeneutic of self-involvement, 91
Hezekiah, 76, 79
hidden polemics, 25, 30, 89
history, 25
history of religion, 23
Holy Spirit, 2
homiletics, 16
horse, 83
hôy, 72
hubris, 36–37
humility, 37
hunger, 73

idols, 25, 47–59, 61, 65
illocution, 90
illustration, 10, 71, 86–87, 89
impatience, 84
implicit disputation speech, 71
incomparability, 17
in-group vision, 6
irony, 51

Jehu, 80
Jerusalem, 78
Jethro, 38–39, 41, 53
judgment, 44, 47, 58, 65, 68, 73, 75, 76, 81, 84, 89

king, 44, 57–58, 61, 77, 80, 87, 92
knowledge, 55, 69, 86

language, 21, 33, 35, 50, 67
lawsuit, 1–3, 1–3, 20, 71
lethargy, 79
letter, xv, 11, 21, 87
liberal tradition, 7, 16
life-skill, 69
literary genre, 19–21, 26, 71
living God, 17, 25
lo' -' ēl, 47

magician, 39

Marduk, 58
materialism, 48
Mesopotamia, 36
method, xv, 15–16, 18–19, 23–24, 29, 88
Milcom, 57
miracle, xiii, 10, 41, 86
missiology, vii–viii, xiii
Moab, 44, 57
mockery, 26, 31, 37–38, 54, 62, 81, 86, 89
modernists, 7, 15, 20
Mot, 49
multiplex-canonical approach, 24
mythology, 33–34

name, 37
narrative, 31
narrative apologetics, 36–47, 89
national deity, 45
natural theology, 34
nature, 25
Nebo, 53, 58
Nebuchadnezzar, 39, 62, 77
New Testament, xiii–xv, 2–3, 19–21, 89
Nile, 38
not-god, 47

oath, 74
obedience, 37, 77, 84
offense, 4, 18, 21
oppression, 66
organizing principle, 24
Osiris, 38

parable, 71
performative utterance, 90
permission of God, 48, 84
Persia, 44
Pharaoh, 38–39, 41, 86
Philistines, 42
philosophical theology, 8, 14–16
philosophy, 16, 17

philosophy of religion, 9, 13, 21
pious fraud, 63
place, 78
plagues of Egypt, 37–43, 53, 86
Plausibilisierung, 5
polemical language, 33, 35
polemics, 8, 10, 17, 23, 25, 31–35, 89
polytheism, 34
practical atheism, 64, 74
practical theology, 8, 10, 13, 15, 18
practice of defense, 19
pragmatism, 84
prayer, 61, 86–87, 91
prediction, 56
presence of God, 43, 73, 75, 79
priest, 27, 38, 41, 57, 86–87
primeval history, 36–37, 73
proclamation, 61
prolegomena, 11–12, 14–15
promise, 76–77, 82–83
proof, 5
prophecy, 10, 56, 82–83, 89
prophetic apologetics, 47–59
prosperity, 64
proverb, 65, 76, 84
provision, 32, 45, 73

queen of heaven, 45, 84
quotation, 70–85, 87

Ra/Re, 38
Rabshakeh, 86–87
reason, 12
Rechenschaftsablage, 5, 11, 13
recognition formula, 39
religious internal pluralism, 22
removal of obstacles, 5
report, 70–85
responsibility, 73, 79
retorsio argumenti, 79
revelation, 10–12, 25, 65
rîb, 3
righteous, 66–69, 75
righteousness, 75, 83

royal ideology, 37
rûaḥ, 52, 53

salvation, 45, 81–82, 89
salvation history, 45
scientific prose, 33
sea, 32, 43
sea monsters, 32
self-assertion, 14
self-assurance, 63, 68
self-confidence, 80
selfishness, 78
semantics, 3, 6
sensory perception, 47, 52–53,
   63–65, 67–68, 75
Septuagint, 3
Shechem, 42
Shemaiah, 80
side track issue, 12
snake, 72
social laws, 74
sociology, 6
sovereignty, 17, 49, 62
speech-act theory, 90–92
spirit, 52, 53
spy, 73
stars, 31, 33
story, 46
strategy, 29, 43, 72, 82, 89
Streitgespräch, 70
success, 68, 69
suffering, 63, 65, 66
superiority, 6, 9, 16, 38, 61, 68
superpowers, 44
syncretism, 22
synonyms, 3

tabernacle, 31
təhôm, 32
temple, 31, 77–79, 87
temptation, 72
ten (number), 40
ten commandments, 41
testimony, 61, 62

Subject Index

theodicy, 65
thirst, 73
Tiamat, 32
Torah, 28, 72, 78–79
trial, 1–3, 20, 63, 71–72
truth claims, 18

unbelief, 12
unfaithfulness, 44, 74, 83
universalism, 34

vapor, 47, 54
vision, 62
vocation, 73

warrior, 43
weakness, 54, 73, 79, 84

weather, 43, 53
Weltentwurf, 34
wicked, 65–69, 75
wilderness, 28, 45, 54, 73
will of God, 84
wisdom, 26, 49, 69, 78, 80, 88
Wissenschaftsprosa, 33
woe [to], 72
world concept, 34
worldview, 35, 89
wrath, 52, 54, 81

year of remission, 74

Scripture Index

Genesis

1–11	36–37
1:1–2:3	29–35
1:2	32
1:14–19	31
1:21	32
1:26–28	31
3:1, 4–5	72
4:9	73
11:4	37, 73
12:2	37
18	83
41:24	38
41:8	38

Exodus

5–12	86
5:2	67
6:7	39
6:27–18:27	39
7:5, 17	39
7:11–12, 22	38
8:3, 14	38
8:10, 22	39
9:11	38
9:14, 29	39
9:22–25	43
10:2	39
11:7	40
12:12	38
12:26–27	91
13:14–15	91
14:4–30	40
14:11–12	45, 73
15:8–12	43
15:11	38
15:24	40
16:3	45, 73
16:3–27	40
17:3	40, 45, 73
17:7	73
18:11	38, 40, 41, 53
19:16–19	43
20:3	41
29:46	40
31:13	40
32	40, 83
32:12	45, 73
34:28	41
39:32–43	31

Leviticus

18	42
18:3	42
23:43	40

Numeri

11:1, 4	40
14:16	45, 73
14:22, 34	40
16:28, 30	40
33:4	38

Deuteronomy

1:27	45, 74
1:31	54
4:6–8	44
4:6	74
4:19	48
4:28	47
4:35	48
4:39	48
5:7	41
6:20–25	91
7:17	74
9:2	74
9:28	45, 66, 73, 74
12:30	42, 74
13:1–5	23
13:2–4	55
13:3	90
15:9	74
16:18–18:22	28
17:3	48
17:17	44
18:21–22	xiv
18:22	56, 91
28:1–14	xiv
29:19	74
31:17–18	74
31:21	47
32:21	54
32:27	45, 73
32:39	49
33:26	43

Joshua

2:9–11	xiv
4:6, 21–24	91
7:9	45
10:11	43
24:2	42
24:14–17	42

Judges

2:11–23	44
5:4–5	43
6:31	47
7:10	43
11:12–27	86
12:16–18	43

1 Samuel

2:2	43, 48
2:10	43
2:30	xiv
4:8	43
5	42
5:3–5	54
6:5–6	43
17:43–47	86

2 Samuel

7:22	48

1 Kings

6:38	31
7:51	31
8:29–35	78
17:24	xiv
18:21–37	86
18:26–29	39
18:27	54
18:39	xiv

20:23, 28	xiv	**Job**	
22:19–23	56	1:9	68
		5:8	68
		8:5ff	68
2 Kings		9:24	66
2:13	xiv	11:13ff	68
9:11	80	12:2ff	68
17:7–23	44	13:7, 10	63
18–19	86	21:14–15	67
19:15, 19	48	21:14	67
19:18	47	22:13–14, 17	67
20:19	76	24:15	68, 75
22:8	80	28:28	69
23:26–27	44	31:24–28	48
24:2–4	44	34:9	67
		35:3	67
1 Chronicles		**Psalms**	
12:18	76	3:3	66
16:26	48	9:12	61
17:20	48	10:1–11	66
		10:4–11	75
Ezra		10:4	68
4:2–22	87	10:11	74
5:3–17	87	14:1	68, 74, 75
6:6–12	87	18:5–20, 32	43
7:12–26	87	18:26	xiv
		18:50	61, 91
		22:8–9	66
		25:2	91
Nehemiah		29:1	58
2:19–20	87	29:3–10	43
3:33–38	87	35:21, 25	74
6:1–14	87	42:4, 11	66
9:6	48	47:2	61
		53:2	68
		57:10	61, 91
Esther		58:2	58
		59:8	67, 74, 75
	62	64:6–7	67, 75
		66:8	61
		71:11	74

Psalms (continued)

73:11	74, 75
78:19–20	74
78:19	45
79:10	66, 75
82:2–5	58
82:6–8	59
82:7	48
86:8	61
86:10	48
89:6–7	58
89:7	61
94:7	67, 74, 75
95:3	61
96:3, 7–10	61
96:4–5	61
96:5	48, 50
97:6–9	61
97:7	61
105:1	61
108:4	61, 91
115	49
115:2–8	52
115:4–8	xiv
115:2	66, 75
117:1	61
119:42–43, 46	61
119:42, 46	92
135	49
135:5–7	53
135:5	61
135:15–18	xiv, 53
135:15–17	51
135:17	52
137:3, 7	74
139:11–12	74

Proverbs

1:7	69
9:10	69
12:15	69
15:33	69
26:12	69
30:9	67

Isaiah

2:18, 20	57
5:1–7	71
5:19	84
7:12	79
9:9	81
9:11, 16	81
9:20	81
13–23	22
19:1	57
21:9	58
22:13	71
24–27	49
28:9–13	82
28:9–10, 14–19	71
28:15	81
28:23–29	71
29:9–14	79
29:10	79
30:9–11	82
30:10	57
30:11	67
30:15–16	64, 83
30:16	71
36–37	86
36:3–4	54
37	xiv
37:16, 20	48
39:8	79
40:12–31	49
40:18–20	xiv
40:20	54
40:27–31	71
40–55	33
41:6–29	xiv
41:6–7, 21–29	49
41:7	54
41:21–23	56
41:23–24	55
42:8–9, 17	49
42:9	56

Isaiah (continued)

43:12	56
43:26	xiv
44:9–11	55
44:9–20	xiv, 49, 51
44:12	54
44:16–17	51
44:20	55
45:14–21	49
45:20–21	xiv
45:20	53
45:21	56
46:1–7	49
46:1–2, 7	53
46:1	58
46:2, 7, 10	xiv
46:10	56
47:10	64
48:3–5	49
48:14	56
49:14–25	71
49:23	xiv
57:19	76

Jeremiah

2:23	72
2:25	83
2:31	80
2:34–35	75
3:6	78
5:12	65, 75
5:19	84
6:14	76
6:16–17	80
7:3–20	78
7:4, 10	78
8:2	48
8:7–9	78
8:8–9	71
8:10–11	56
8:11	76
10	49
10:1–16	49, 50
10:4	54
10:5	52
10:6–8	50
10:6	53
10:9–12	50
10:11, 15	57
10:13	53
10:14–15	54
10:14	52
11:19, 21	82
12:1	3
12:4	64, 75
14:13–18	56
14:13	78
14:22	xiv
16:19–20	48
17:15	65, 80
18:12	64, 81, 83
18:18	28
20:10	81
20:11–18	81
20:12	3
21:13	78
22:21	80
23:17–31	82
23:17	76
23:6	82
23:9–40	56, 82
23:9, 17	83
26–27	51
26:26–27	80
27:9–16	77
27:11–12	77
28	56, 86
28:2–4	77
28:11	77
29:15	75
31:6	3
31:29–30	71, 84
33:23–26	71
43:12	57
44	46
44:16–19	84

Jeremiah (continued)

44:17–18	46
46–51	22
46:25	57
48:7, 13	57
49:1, 3	58
50:2	58
51:18	57
51:44	58

Lamentations

2:14	56
5:7	84

Ezekiel

6:6	57
7:26	28
8:12	65, 75
9:9	65, 75
11:2–17	71
12:21–28	71
12:22–28	76
12:22, 27	79
12:24	56
13	56
13:2	82
13:34, 38	82
18:1–20	71
18:2, 25, 29	83
18:23	84
18:25, 29	65
18:32	84
20:32–44	71
30:13	57
33:10–29	71
37:11–13	71

Daniel

1–6	86
2:2–12	39
2:27–28	39
2:47	62
3:16–18	63
3:28–33	62
4:31–34	62
6:26–27	62

Hosea

9:7	80
10:3	65

Joel

2:17	65

Amos

1–2	22
3:2	79
5:18–20	71
9:10	76

Jonah

	22

Micah

2:6	75
3:5–8	57
3:11	79
7:10	65, 75, 80

Habakkuk

2:4	52
2:18–19	49
2:18	xiv
2:19	52
3:2, 5–9	52

Scripture Index

Zephaniah

1:12	65, 75
1:5	48
2:4–15	22
2:11	57
3:4	56

Haggai

1:2–11	71
1:5–11	85
1:9	84

Zechariah

13:2, 4	56
13:2	57

Malachi

2:17	65, 84
3:14–15	64, 67

Matthew

7:22–23	20
12:10	2
27:12	2
27:24	20

Mark

3:2	2
11:29	2
14:60–61	2
15:2–4	2

Luke

6:7	2
12:11	2
13:26–27	20
17:20	2
21:14	2
23:2–14	2
23:3, 9	2

John

1:21	2
5:45	2
8:6	2
18:29	2

Acts

4:7–12	20
5:28–32	20
19:33	2
22:1–21	20
22:1, 30	2
23:1–6	20
24:2–19	2
24:10–21	20
25:8	20
25:16–19	2
26:1–2	21
26:1–24	2, 20

Romans

2:15	2
9	21
11	21

1 Corinthians

9:3	2

2 Corinthians

5:11	5
7:11	2
12:19	2

Philippians

1:7, 16 — 2

2 Timothy

4:16 — 2

1 Peter

3:15 — xiv, 2, 91, 92